MW01295830

Logic Primer

Elihu Carranza, Ph.D.

Inky Publication

Logic Primer

Published by Inky Publications

Napa, California

Copyright © 2012 Elihu Carranza

ISBN-10: 1479116378

ISBN-13: 978-1479116379

SOLI DEO GLORIA

Logic is defined is "the science of necessary inference," from Gordon H. Clark. He locates the biblical origin of logic in John 1:1, the necessary inference being: Logic Is God. "In the beginning was Logic, and Logic was with God, and Logic was God.... In Logic was life and the life was the light of men." (*Logic*, Gordon H. Clark; The Trinity Foundation, p. 115 [HC ed.])

.

CONTENTS

ACKNOWLEDGMENTS

Thanks to Anil Bharvaney (who subsequently perished in the World Trade Center attack) and James McAnany for their valuable comments and suggestions. A special note of gratitude is due to Gordon H. Clark from whom I have learned much about philosophy, theology, and logic. His books, kept in print by the late Dr. John W. Robbins and now by Thomas W. Juodaitis, both of the Trinity Foundation in Unicoi, Tennessee, 37692, are a God-granted source of intellectual ammunition for all who seek knowledge and truth. My wife deserves a special note of recognition and gratitude. Her labor of patience and concern for clarity and accuracy improved the manuscript substantially. Without her assistance, there simply would be no *Logic Primer*

1 DEFINITIONS

A question sometimes asked is "What is logic?" to which the standard reply usually begins with a definition of logic such as, "Logic is the science of necessary inference." This Primer will spell out the answer to this question in some detail. However, for a start, logic is about laws (axioms or principles), propositions, inference, arguments, and the validity of arguments. Of course, there is much more that falls beyond the scope of a primer. Other related questions will receive relevant commentary as the subject develops.

Three laws of logic, also known as the three laws of thought, govern necessary inference of a conclusion from premises. These laws are universal, irrefutable, and true. Indeed, without these laws, it is difficult, if not impossible, to imagine how anything at all could be intelligible. These laws or axioms are the basis of necessary inference; without them, there is no necessary inference. Moreover, necessary inference of a conclusion from premises presupposes that the laws of logic are universal, irrefutable, and true. By "universal," we mean allow for no exception. "Irrefutable" means that any attempt to refute them makes use of them, thus establishing them as necessary for argument. "True" means not only "not-false," but also not false, because their ground is the Logos of God, the source and determiner of all truth. Furthermore, the laws stand together as a trinity. To fault one is to fault all, and to uphold one upholds the others. Together, these laws establish and clarify the meaning of necessary inference for logic. The three laws of logic set forth in summary fashion include commentary to make clear their significance.

The Law of Identity

The law of identity states that if any statement is true, then it is true; or, every proposition implies itself: *a implies a*. This may appear to be trivial, but as Gordon Clark notes, what a strange world it would be if it were not the case, for it would be a world without the concept of identity or sameness.

The Law of Excluded Middle

The law of excluded middle states that everything must either be or not be; or, everything is *a or not-a*. That is to say, for example, a rock is either hard or not hard, or either at rest or not-at rest. What can be said of a passenger in an airplane en route to a far-away place? Is he at rest or not at rest? Both at rest and not at rest? Obviously, not both. One cannot have it both ways at the same time or place or in the same respect. The passenger, if seated, is at rest in respect to the aircraft, but in motion with respect to the earth.

The Law of Contradiction

The law of contradiction (also known as the law of non-contradiction) states that no statement can be both true and false; or, *a and not*-a is a contradiction -- always false; thus, *not both a and not-a*. It states that nothing can both be and not be at the same time and at the same place. Aristotle's formulation of this law states that the same attribute cannot at the same time belong and not belong to the same subject and in the same respect: *Not both a and not-a*. Again, every statement of the form *a and not-a* is false. Every such compounded statement is contradictory.

For example, "Therefore, *there is* now no condemnation for those who are in Christ Jesus" (Romans 8:1a) cannot be both true and false. To assert that the statement and its denial are both true or both false at the same time and in the same respect is to fall into contradiction and absurdity.

The law of contradiction is supreme; it encompasses the other two. Its formulation as *Not both a and not-a* assumes the Law of Identity in that the proposition "a" univocally implies itself (*a implies a*). As a disjunction, it expresses the Law of Excluded Middle, *a or not-a*. Furthermore, the Law of Contradiction is necessary for any meaningful discourse, for without it, the distinction between truth and falsity disappears and with it, meaning.

John Robbins nailed it thus:

"The law of contradiction means something more. It means that every word in the sentence 'The line is straight' has a specific meaning. *The* does not mean *any*, *all*, or *no*. *Line* does not mean *dog, dandelion*, or *doughnut*. *Is* does not mean *is not*. *Straight* does not mean *white*, or anything else. Each word has a definite meaning. In order to have a definite meaning, a word must not only mean something, it must also not mean something. *Line* means *line*, but it also does not mean *not-line, dog, sunrise*, or *Jerusalem*. If *line* were to mean everything, it would mean nothing; and no one, including you, would have the foggiest idea what you mean when you say the word *line*. The law of contradiction means that each word, to have a meaning, must also not mean something." (John W. Robbins. "Why Study Logic," *Trinity Review*, Jul/Aug 1985, No. 44)

These laws apply not only to the unambiguous, precise terms contained in the propositions of arguments, but also to the words of all meaningful discourse. Without the first, identity or sameness is lost; without the second, confusion begins; and without the last, nonsense is in full residence. Without them intelligible discourse is impossible.

Propositions

Logic is most certainly about propositions. A proposition is a form of words in which the predicate is affirmed or denied of the subject. More simply, It is the meaning expressed by a declarative sentence. (Gordon H. Clark. *Logic*, HC ed., p. 131). Declarative sentences are either true or false, a property essential to propositions. Other sentences, in expressing commands, posing questions, or conveying exhortations are neither true nor false. Some questions, rhetorical questions, are intended as propositions. If a question is indeed rhetorical, then it is neither true nor false.

The illustration of proposition most often used is one in which sentences taken from different languages are seen to have the same meaning. *IL pleut; Es regnet; Esta lluviendo* mean the same thing: *It is raining.*

The proposition expressed in these following sentences is the same meaning:

(1) Jesus told Nicodemus "except a man be born again, he cannot see the kingdom of God."

(2) Nicodemus was told by Jesus "except a man be born again, he cannot see the kingdom of God."

The subject and predicate names have been interchanged and "told" replaced by "was told by," but the meaning is the same.

Thus, simply stated, a proposition is the meaning of a declarative sentence.

Premises and Conclusions

Propositions are the premises and conclusions of arguments. In ordinary language arguments, it is not always apparent which propositions are premises and which are conclusions. For one thing, in some arguments the conclusion is unstated. In another twist, even if the conclusion is explicit, its position is not always last in a series of propositions; it may be stated first, or in the middle of a series of premises. As an examination of the well-known argument about Socrates, men, and mortals will demonstrate, a conclusion can come first, in the middle, or last.

First: "It follows that Socrates is mortal, because all men are mortal, and Socrates is a man."

Second, in the middle: "All men are mortal, so Socrates is a mortal, for he is a man."

Third, the traditional formulation is the most familiar with the conclusion "Socrates is mortal" as the last statement and the other two serving as premises.

A good strategy: First, identify the conclusion of an argument, and then identify the premises intended to establish the conclusion.

Necessary Inference

In logic, when we speak of making an inference, we do not mean guesses or forecasts, no matter how educated the guess or forecast. Inference means the derivation of logical consequences from the premises of an argument. An inference is a necessary inference when a conclusion follows logically, strictly, from premises. In other words, if premises imply a certain conclusion logically, then the inference from premises to conclusion is a necessary inference. Examples abound, but to remain on familiar territory, take this mini-lesson in geography:

If Canada lies north of the United States, and the United States of America is north of Mexico, then it follows, logically that Canada is north of Mexico. That is to say, the statement "Canada is north of Mexico" is a necessary inference derived from the premises.

To see that it is the *form* of the argument that is important and the reference to geography inconsequential, substitute *A* for *Canada*, *B* for the *United States* and *C* for *Mexico*. The conclusion "A is north of C" follows necessarily from (1) A is north of B, and (2) B is north of C. The conclusion is a necessary inference or consequence of the other two statements taken in conjunction.

Argument

As a first attempt, we can define argument as a series of connected propositions in support of another proposition or position. Those propositions offered in support of another one are known as the premises. The proposition assumed to follow from the premises is the conclusion of the argument.

A simpler formulation: an argument is a set of premises in support of a conclusion; however, the phrase "in support of," being a figurative expression, may prove to be problematic. Of course, there is a relation in an argument between the premises and conclusion, but the relation we have in mind is a logical relation.

Thus, a better formulation of the definition is this: an argument consists of propositions from which another proposition, the conclusion, can be derived or deduced as a necessary consequence. The connected series of statements, the propositions, are reasons intended to establish a conclusion or position. The conclusion is implicit in the premises and is deduced from the combined premises alone. Thus, the necessary inference we have in mind is a deductive inference, for the conclusion is deduced from the premises.

To add to our previous example using geography, here is another simple deduction using arithmetic: If 10 is greater than 5, and 5 is greater than 1, what can be deduced about the relation of 10 and 1? What statement is a necessary consequence of the two statements? The reader should be able to not only deduce the correct mathematical proposition from the previous propositions, but also understand that *necessary consequence* and valid *deductive inference* denote the same thing. The deduction of conclusions from premises is at the heart of logic.

Indicator Words

Arguments include such phrases or words as "it follows that," "because," "for," "and," "so." These words, known as indicator words or phrases, introduce or otherwise indicate the presence of a premise or premises and a conclusion. We distinguish between those indicator words or phrases that either introduce premises or join them together, and those that introduce conclusions. The former are labeled premise indicators, the latter, conclusion indicators. A brief list of some of the more common indicator words follows:

Premises	Conclusions
... and ...	so
... but ...	thus
since ...	it follows
nevertheless ...	hence
because ...	therefore
assuming that ...	accordingly
however ...	consequently
inasmuch as ...	it follows that
this is why ...	which means that
implied by ...	one can conclude that
inasmuch as ...	from which we deduce that

Validity

Just above, mention was made of deducing conclusions from premises. Given an argument, an individual may claim that from some premises, a conclusion seems to follow. One may ask whether the conclusion is a necessary consequence of these premises. If indeed the conclusion follows necessarily from the stated premises, then we have an instance of a valid argument. Validity, however, does not establish the truth of the propositions, only that given these premises, this conclusion follows necessarily. Stated in another way, we say "the premises of this argument necessarily imply the conclusion of this argument; therefore, the argument is valid."

On the other hand, if a person's claim of logical necessity between premises and conclusion fails, the argument is invalid. Every deductive argument, so defined, is either valid or invalid: if not valid, then invalid. If an argument is not invalid, then it is valid.

If a deductive argument is valid, it may be either sound or unsound. If all of the propositions of the argument are true, it is sound, otherwise, unsound -- yet valid. Sound and unsound are qualities of valid deductive arguments only; they never apply to invalid arguments.

Summary

The laws of logic, the law of identity (a implies a); the law of excluded middle (a or not-a); and the law of non-contradiction (not both a and not-a) govern necessary inferences. Without these laws, there is no science of necessary inference and nothing intelligible at all. Logic, as the systematic study of necessary inference, has to do with arguments. The arguments consist of propositions, the meanings of declarative sentences. Propositions are either true or false. Such propositions function as premises and conclusions of deductive arguments. If the relation between the premises and conclusion of an argument expresses a necessary inference, the argument is valid. If, on examination, an argument fails the test of necessary consequence, the argument is invalid. Deductive arguments are either valid or invalid; if valid, the argument is either sound or unsound. A valid argument is sound when all of its propositions are true, otherwise, unsound. How one determines necessary inference, or how an argument qualifies as valid or invalid is the subject matter of the remaining chapters of this Primer.

Review

1. In a paragraph or two, What is logic? Begin your written account with the definition: "Logic is ...," then explain each of the terms in the definiens (the predicate of the definition).

2. What are the three laws of logic? Can you explain their significance for necessary inference? How do the laws of logic govern necessary inference?

3. In a brief paragraph, explain why the following language does not qualify as a proposition, as written: "Thou shalt have no other gods before me." Reword the language, such that it constitutes a proposition. (Hint: convert the sentence into a true declarative sentence.)

4. Illustrate deductive inference. How does deductive inference differ from a guess or a forecast?

5. Suppose a car's starter fails to turn over when the ignition is activated. What, if anything, can be concluded?

Exercise 1.1 True/False on Definitions

Instructions: Which of the following is true and which is false? If a statement is false, reword it to qualify as a true.

	STATEMENTS	T/F
1	Logic is the systematic study and knowledge of necessary inference.	
2	Logic is sometimes irrelevant to intelligible conversation or discussion.	
3	The Law of Identity states that a statement is either true or false.	
4	The Law of Excluded Middle states that a or not-a is true.	
5	The Law of Contradiction states that a and not-a is always false.	
6	"Thou shalt not kill" is an example of a proposition.	

7	A proposition is the meaning of a declarative sentence.	
8	Necessary inference of a conclusion from premises is a requirement of validity in arguments.	
9	A deductive argument consists of premises from which it is claimed the conclusion logically follows.	
10	Every valid deductive argument is an example of a sound argument.	

Exercise 1.2 Correct Definitions

Instructions: Fill in the blanks in each item with the letter of the most correct answer. If no correct answer is listed, choose " l " None of the Above.

a	logic	g	invalid
b	law of identity	h	valid
c	proposition	i	law of contradiction
d	premise	j	unsound
e	sound	k	law of excluded middle
f	necessary inference	l	None of the Above

	STATEMENTS	
1	_____ is the science of necessary inference.	
2	_____ states that a proposition always implies itself, a implies a.	
3	_____ states that a and not-a is always and everywhere false.	
4	Without _____ all intelligible conversation and discussion vanishes.	
5	_____ is a logical relation between premises and	

	conclusions in valid arguments.	
6	"If X is greater than Y, and Y is greater than Z; then X is greater than Z." is a _____ argument.	
7	Which of the three laws of logic is said to be supreme since it embraces the other two? _____ .	
8	If a valid argument is classified as _____ some of its propositions are false.	
9	In logic, deductive argument is not classified as true or false but as _____ or _____.	
10	A valid argument is classified as _____ if all its propositions are true.	
11	A valid argument is either _____ or _____.	
12	Either a or not-a expresses _____,	

2 PROPOSITIONS

Propositions are classified as either standard form or nonstandard. We first consider the four standard form propositions, then discuss nonstandard propositions in the last section of this chapter.

Each standard form consists of a subject and a predicate. In each form, the subject and the predicate are joined together by *is* or *are*, the *copula*. Thus, the propositions of syllogistic reasoning consist of *subject-copula-predicate* combinations and whatever quantifying relationship is required: *All*, *No*, *Some*, or *Some — not—*. Where *a* and *b* stand for the subject and predicate terms, respectively, these criteria yield four forms:

(1) All a is b.

(2) No a is b.

(3) Some a is b.

(4) Some a is not b.

The Four Forms

Syllogistic reasoning makes use of four and only four types of proposition, or four forms. For this reason, but not this reason alone, the word *form* has special significance. The word indicates that in logic we pay more attention to the form than the content of an argument. The diverse subject matter of arguments is not relevant for determining their validity or invalidity. To repeat: It is the form of the argument that determines its validity. The form (or outline, or skeleton) of an argument is made explicit by means of its propositional forms.

The A Form

The proposition "All men are mortal" asserts a relation of inclusion between the class of men and the class of mortals. More plainly, it states that all members of the class *men* fall within the class *mortal.* The form of all such propositions is *All a is b*, where *a* stands for the subject and *b* stands for the predicate. The form of an A proposition can be expressed even more succinctly as *A(ab)*. Note that in A propositions, the subject is included in the predicate, but not the predicate in the subject. From "All men are mortals" it does not follow that all mortals are men. Animals, for instance, are mortal, and by biblical account, animals are not men. (For a discussion of the definition of "all," see Clark's *Logic*, HC ed., pp. 81-83.)

The E Form

The proposition "No Christian is an atheist" asserts a relation of exclusion between two classes, Christians and atheists. No member of the class *Christians* is a member of the class *atheists*, and conversely, no atheist is a Christian. The classes of E propositions are mutually exclusive. The form is *No a is b*, or *E(ab)*, where *a* stands for any subject, and *b* stands for any predicate. Thus, with E propositions all members of one class are excluded from the other, and *vice versa.*

The I Form

The proposition "Some Americans are Calvinists" asserts a relation of partial inclusion between the class *Americans* and the class *Calvinists.* Something less than all members of the subject-class is included in the predicate-class, and conversely, some members of the class Calvinists are included in the class Americans. The form of the I proposition is *Some a is b*, or I(ab), where, as before, *a* stands for any subject, *b* for any predicate.

Ordinarily, *some* can mean a few in number; in logic, the word can also mean as few as one.

The O Form

The proposition "Some men are not Christian" asserts a relation of partial exclusion between the two classes, *men* and *Christians.* Some men are entirely excluded from all of the class of Christians. The form of the O proposition is *Some a is not b*, or O(ab). Does it follow then that some Christians are not men? No, the converse of an O proposition does not follow from the original. Remember, there is no converse for O propositions.

The following chart serves as a summary of the foregoing four forms. Do not be confused in that the letters *a* and *b* are used throughout, even when the propositions contain different subject matter. Recall that the letters, *a* and *b*, stand for any subject and any predicate, respectively. Indeed, we could have used *x* and *y* or any other pair of letters to stand for subjects and predicates.

Chart 2.1: Four Forms

All men are mortal.	All a is b.	A(ab)
No Christian is an atheist.	No a is b.	E(ab)
Some Americans are Calvinists.	Some a is b.	I(ab)
Some men are not Christian.	Some a is not b.	O(ab)

The source of the letters for the four forms is of historical interest. From the Latin *affirmo,* meaning affirmative in quality, we have the A and I forms; the E and O forms come from *nego,* meaning negative in quality.

Formal Properties of the Forms

There are three formal characteristics shared by the four forms altogether: distribution, quality and quantity, -- each defined just below.

Distribution

The formal properties, quality and quantity, of A, E, I, and O forms depend on the distribution of the subject and predicate terms. We distinguish a distributed term (subject or predicate) from an undistributed term in this manner: a distributed term is one modified by All or No; otherwise, the term is undistributed. Using "d" for distributed and "u" for undistributed, the four forms distribute their terms as indicated below in Chart 2.2.

Chart 2.2: Distribution

FORMS		Subject Term	Predicate Term
A	All s $_d$ is p $_u$	Distributed	Undistributed
E	No s $_d$ is p $_d$.	Distributed	Distributed
I	Some s $_u$ is p $_u$.	Undistributed	Undistributed
O	Some s $_u$ is not p $_d$.	Undistributed	Distributed

Where, s = subject term and p = predicate term.

The chart is no substitute for memorizing the definition of distribution and understanding what distribution means. The importance of distribution cannot be overemphasized, for it not only serves as the basis for defining the quality and quantity of the four forms, but also is a necessary element in determining the validity of deductive inference in syllogisms, as we shall see. For emphasis, a review and summary of the discussion on distribution is set forth in Chart 2.3.

Chart 2.3: Distribution Descriptions

FORM	DESCRIPTION
A Form	Only the subject term is distributed; the predicate is undistributed since, as noted, all of the predicate is not included in the subject.
E Form	Subjects and predicates in E forms are mutually exclusive; thus, both are distributed.
I Form	Some part of the subject class is included in some part of the predicate class and *vice versa*; therefore, both terms are undistributed.
O Form	Only the predicate term is distributed, the subject term undistributed, since some part of the subject class is excluded from all of the predicate class.

Quality

Previously we indicated that the A and I letters came from the Latin *affirmo*, and E and O from the Latin *nego*. Remembering the source of the letters may help to recall that the A and I forms are affirmative in quality; E and O, negative in quality. An affirmative form is one that does not distribute its predicate. The A and I forms do not distribute the predicates; therefore, they are affirmative in quality. A negative form is one that distributes its predicate. The E and O forms distribute the predicates; therefore, negative in quality.

Quantity

Each of the four forms is either universal or particular in quantity. If a form distributes its subject term, it is universal in quantity. The A and E forms are universal, since each distributes its subject term. On the other hand, a form is particular in quantity if its subject term is undistributed. The I and the O forms have undistributed subject terms; therefore, they are particular in quantity.

Non-standard Propositions

The requirement that standard form propositions only may be present in the premises and conclusion of syllogisms may result in some perhaps awkward formulations of English. In the case of an English verb other than the present tense of the verb *to be*, change the verb into a predicate adjective. For example, "All competent students know logic" becomes "All competent students are knowers-of-logic." When the language of the sentence contains clauses or prepositional phrases as well as a verb other than the English copula, the use of parameters will help make the sense of the proposition clear. For example, "All persons-who-are-competent-students are persons-who-are-knowers-of-logic." Here the word "persons" appears in both the subject and predicate, and together with hyphens assists in reading the proposition as an A proposition. The purpose is to make the sense of the proposition clear.

Exclusive and Exceptive Propositions

More effort is required with two other classes of propositions: exclusive and exceptive propositions. How can we make clear the sense of this exclusive proposition? "Only atheists will be ejected." Ask yourself, "What does it mean?" It means, "All persons-who-are-ejected are persons-who-are-atheists." Thus the sense of exclusive propositions (only x is y) is the A Form, the result obtained when subject and predicate are interchanged. Exceptive propositions (all except x is y) are really two in one form. For example, "All except the soldiers gave up the fight" means (1) All persons who were non-soldiers (civilians) are persons who gave up the fight; and (2) No person who was a soldier is a person who gave up the fight. Note that neither one of these can be deduced from the other. They are two different forms, each of which must receive individual treatment if the original exceptive proposition is a premise in an argument.

Propositions with Proper Names

Some propositions make use of proper names as in the familiar men, mortals, and Socrates syllogism. Some logic texts label propositions with proper names: singular propositions. We make no distinction between singular and other universal propositions. All propositions using proper names are either A or E, depending on the quality. The name Socrates, in "Socrates is mortal" is the entire subject class, which happens to have only one member. An example of an E form is "Socrates is not immortal," or, "No Socrates is immortal." Some propositions appear to name only some members of a class, when all members of a class are either included or excluded. Example: "Dinosaurs are extinct" does not mean that some are, or some may not be, extinct. The sense of the statement is that all dinosaurs are extinct. In other words, the "all" is implied, and when the context calls for or implies "all" or "no," the result is either an A Form or an E Form, depending on the quality of the original.

Logical versus Grammatical Subjects

Grammatical and logical subjects sometimes need to be distinguished if one is to achieve the correct sense of a proposition. Clark provides an example: "You always squirm out of an argument." The grammatical subject, "you," is not the logical subject. Rather, *always* meaning, "every time you get into an argument" is the logical subject. The sense of the original is:

"All TIMES-you-get-into-an-argument are TIMES-you-squirm-out-of-it."

Similar treatment is required for "Jones always wins at tennis." The logical subject is what the statement is about. The proposition does not assert that Jones is at all times (24/7) winning at tennis. The more reasonable meaning is that Jones wins at tennis WHENEVER he plays.

"All TIMES when Jones plays tennis are TIMES when he wins at tennis."

The parameter "times" is useful for uniform translation into standard form.

Two more examples follow:

(1) Smith loses a sale whenever he is sick.

(2) Where there is no vision, the people perish.

The first translates into "All TIMES in which Smith is sick are TIMES in which Smith loses a sale." The second translates "All INSTANCES where there is no vision are INSTANCES where the people perish."

Note however, that in the proposition "Time flies," "time" is both the grammatical and logical subject. ("Flies" is both the grammatical and logical predicate.) The whole idea of the subject is expressed in the noun "time," and the whole idea of the predicate is expressed by the verb "flies."

The job of re-wording non-standard propositions into standard form A, E, I, and O has benefits beyond the requirements of immediate inference. True, effective application of tests to determine the validity of inference depends on the clear sense of standard form propositions. However, in other contexts where valid inference is not an issue, rewording non-standard into standard forms will avoid misunderstandings, mistakes, and confusion. Remember this: if you cannot put a non-standard proposition into standard form, you actually do not know what it means. What cannot be expressed clearly is ambiguous or not meaningful.

Summary

Standard form propositions consist of subject and predicate terms joined by the copula "is" or "are" and qualified by "All," "No," "Some," or "Some — not —." These requirements yield four forms: (1) All a is b, (2) No a is b, (3) Some a is b, and (4) Some a is not b which are known as A, E, I, and O forms, respectively. These forms are also expressed as A(ab), E(ab), I(ab), and O(ab). The formal properties of distribution, quality, and quantity of the four standard forms were explained and illustrated. A distributed term is one modified by "All" or "No;" otherwise, the term is undistributed. If a proposition's predicate term is distributed, the proposition is negative in quality; if the predicate of a proposition is not distributed, then it is affirmative in quality. This definition of quality distinguishes E(ab) and O(ab), both negative, from A(ab) and I(ab), both affirmative. If a proposition distributes its subject term, it is universal in quantity. On the other hand, if a proposition's subject term is undistributed, it is particular in quantity. By this definition, we distinguish A(ab) and E(ab), both universal, from I(ab) and O(ab), both particular. Finally, some guidelines for translating nonstandard propositions into standard form were described.

Review

1. Of the four standard forms, which distribute their subject terms? Which do not distribute their subject terms? What formal property is defined in each case?

2. Of the four standard forms, which distribute their predicate terms? Which do not distribute their predicate terms? What formal property is defined in each case?

3. Given form A(ab). Which of the other three forms differ in both quantity and quality from A(ab)?

4. What is the general formulation of exclusive propositions? What is the procedure for transforming an exclusive proposition into standard form?

5. Compose some examples of exceptive propositions. Identify the two component sentences embedded in each.

Exercise 2.1 Four Forms

Instructions: Choose the letter of the most correct answer for each of the statements below.

a	A(ab)	g	undistributed
b	I(ab)	h	quantity
c	O(ab)	i	quality
d	E(ab)	j	universal
e	distributed	k	particular
f	redistributed	l	None of the Above

	STATEMENTS	
1	The forms A and E are _____ in quantity.	
2	The forms I and O are _____ in quantity.	
3	If the subject terms of forms are _____ the forms are universal.	
4	If the predicate terms of forms are _____ the forms are affirmative in quality.	
5	If the predicate terms of forms are _____ the forms are negative in quality.	
6	The forms A(ab) and I(ab) are similar in _____ but dissimilar in _____.	
7	The form with both particular quantity and affirmative quality is _____.	
8	The form with both terms undistributed is _____.	
9	The form with a distributed subject term, and an undistributed predicate term is _____.	
10	The form with both terms distributed is _____.	
11	The form A(ab) differs from form _____ in both the distribution of terms, quantity, and quality.	
12	The formal qualities of the forms are defined in terms of whether or not the subjects and predicates of the forms are _____ or _____.	

Exercise 2.2 Translating into Standard Form

Instructions: Rewrite each of the following as standard A, E, I, or O Forms. Use the letters in parentheses for subject and predicate terms for each. (If you cannot put them into standard form, you do not know what they mean.)

	STATEMENTS
1	No Christian is a secularist. (c, s)
2	Some children run to school. (c, s)

3	Only good students get A's. (s, g)
4	None but the brave deserve the fair. (b, f)
5	All except workers may enter. (w, e)
6	Only freshmen need use the back door. (f, b)
7	The poor always ye have with you. (w, p)
8	You always squirm out of an argument. (a, o)
9	Except the Lord build the house, they labor in vain who build it. (h, v)
10	Logic is the science of necessary inference. (l, s)
11	Whosoever committeth sin transgresseth also the law. (s, l)
12	The fall brought humanity into an estate of sin and misery. (f, e)
13	Nothing worthwhile is easy. (w, e)
14	Whoso loveth instruction loveth knowledge. (i, k)
15	There is therefore now no condemnation to those who are in Christ Jesus. (j c)
16	The sacraments of the New Testament are Baptism and the Lord's supper. (s, a)
17	In order to say something meaningful, one must use the law of contradiction. (m, l)
18	Some hold that God's sovereignty and man's responsibility are paradoxical. (s, p)
19	Most of the items in this exercise are easy. (i, e)
20	Fifty percent of eligible voters did not vote. (e, v)

3 IMMEDIATE INFERENCE

In logic, we distinguish two types of deductive inference: immediate inference and mediated inference. An immediate inference occurs in an argument consisting of two propositions: one premise and a conclusion. For example, from the premise "all men are mortal," one can immediately conclude that some men are mortal. The immediate inference involves two and only two terms (men and mortal) whereas mediated inferences (syllogisms) have three and only three terms. Immediate inferences are the subject of this chapter. The next chapter discusses syllogisms.

With both varieties of inference, it is important to distinguish valid from invalid inference.

Valid Inference

An inference counts as valid whenever the form of the conclusion is true every time the forms of the premises are. If the form of the conclusion is not true every time the forms of the premises are true, then the inference is invalid.

Following explications of the Clark Diagram and the Square of Opposition, an analysis of the relations that hold between the Square of Opposition and the Clark Diagram, using the definition of valid inference above and applying it as a rule to a particular case, will be set forth.

The following chart (the content borrowed from Euler, the mathematician, via Clark), shows how many instances a form is true. Five sets of circles correspond to five ways in which two terms (subject and predicate terms) relate in the four forms. The circles, numbered as cases 1 through 5 for easy reference, correspond to the four standard forms.

The "Lines" are of special significance. They represent the number of cases a given form covers. Thus, Form A-Line spans Cases 1 and 2; Form O-Line spans Cases 3, 4, and 5. Form I-Line spans Cases 1, 2, 3, and 4. Form E-Line denotes only one case, Case 5.

Chart 3.1: Clark Diagram
2 Terms Related in 5 Ways.

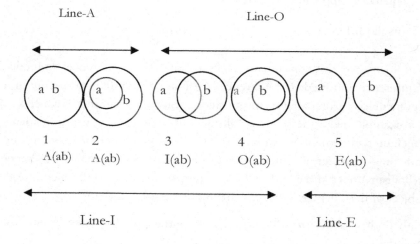

Case 1   One sense of A(ab), where All a is b & All b is a.

Case 2   Another sense of A(ab), where All a is b, but not All b is a.

Case 3   I(ab), Some a is b; & Some b is a.

Case 4   O(ab), Some a is not b.

Case 5   E(ab), No a is b, & No b is a.

To repeat. An inference is valid if the form of the conclusion is true every time the forms of the premises are. In other words, a valid inference from premises to conclusion depends on the arrangement of the subject and predicate being true in the conclusion, every time the arrangement of the same subject and predicate is true in the premises.

Line A designates *All*; Line E designates *No*; Line I designates *Some*; and Line O designates *Some—is not—*. Lines I and O require a bit more concentrated effort to grasp all their cases than Lines A and E.

An inspection of the five sets or cases of circles shows the following.

A(ab), or *All a is b*, is true in two of the five sets of circles: Cases 1 and 2. Line A covers the two cases.

I(ab), *Some a is b*, is true in four sets: Cases 1, 2, 3, and 4; line I spans the four cases.

O(ab), *Some a is not b*, is true three times, in the 3rd, 4th, and 5th Cases, as shown by line O.

E(ab), or *No a is b*, is true only once, in the 5th case, as shown by line E.

Application of the diagram should convince the student of its usefulness. For example, A(ab) logically implies I(ab), since I(ab) is true every time A(ab) is true. Similarly, E(ab) implies O(ab) is a valid inference, since O(ab) is true every time E(ab) is true as an inspection of Chart 3.1 circles and lines O and E show. On the other hand one cannot validly infer from O(ab), the form E(ab), since E(ab) is not true every time O(ab) is true; O(ab) is true three times, E(ab) only once. Similarly, that I(ab) implies A(ab) is not a valid inference, since A(ab) is not true every time I(ab) is true.

Square of Opposition

The valid inferences of the previous paragraph belong to a set of sixteen that are captured in a good memory device, the square of opposition, shown next. Become familiar with the various kinds of opposition shown between the four forms. Keep in mind that the square of opposition does not justify the immediate inferences, but merely displays them in the form of a chart.

Chart 3.2: Square of Opposition

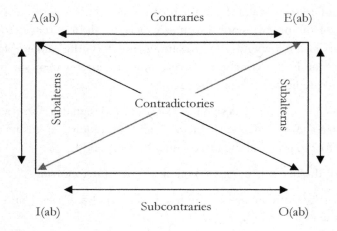

The four relationships are contraries, subcontraries, subalternation, and contradiction. Definitions follow in the order listed with examples.

Contraries

By contraries we mean that the two forms A(ab) and E(ab) cannot both be true together; however, both may be false. Examine Chart 3.1. Note that lines A and E do not overlap which means they cannot both be true in any instance. Since the lines A and E do not exhaust all five cases, they could both be false together. If, for example, some Christians are Calvinists (Case 3 or the third set of circles), then the corresponding A (All Christians are Calvinists) and E (No Christians are Calvinists) are both false.

Subcontraries

The forms, I(ab) and O(ab), are subcontraries, meaning that they cannot both be false together, but they could both be true. Referring again to Chart 3.1, the lines I and O exhaust all 5 cases, and overlap each other to show that they can both be true together -- as in, Some Christians are Calvinists, and Some Christians are not Calvinists.

Subalternations

Subalterns are two forms that are both true together or both false together. There are two pairs of subalterns: (1) A(ab) & I(ab); and (2) E(ab) & O(ab). Chart 3.1 shows that lines A and I are both true under cases 1 and 2, and both false in Case 5. In Case 5, if it is true that No men are angels, then the corresponding A and I are both false. A similar analysis applies to the second pair of subalterns. If, All men are sinners, then the corresponding E and O forms are both false.

(It should be noted here that logic alone does not assert the existence or the nonexistence of anything. The existence or nonexistence of men, sinners, or angels in these propositions, for example, is a matter for history or biology, as Clark suggests, or some other discipline. (Clark, G. H. *Logic*, HC ed., p. 84)

In short, the truth of the A or E includes and necessitates the truth of the I or the O, respectively. From the truth of I or O, we have no right to infer the truth or falsity of the A or E, respectively. However, from the falsity of the I, the falsity of the A is a valid inference, and from the falsity of O, the falsity of E is a valid inference.

Contradiction

The strongest form of opposition is contradiction. Two forms are contradictories, if they cannot both be true together and cannot both be false together. Lines A and O, and E and I can be seen to meet without overlapping in Chart 3.1 and, at the same time, each pair exhausts all cases. A(ab) & O(ab), and E(ab) & I(ab) are contradictories. From the truth (falsity) of an A Form proposition, one can validly infer the falsity (truth) of the related O Form proposition. Similarly, from the truth (falsity)of an E Form proposition, the inference of the falsity (truth) of the related I Form propositions is valid.

As previously mentioned, the square of opposition incorporates a number of useful relationships that hold among the four forms. With it, we can determine, for example, whether the following inference is valid or not: "Since it is the case that all men are mortal; it is false that some men are not mortal." The premise is an A proposition; the conclusion is an O proposition; the A and O forms are contradictories. Another way of stating this valid inference is to say that from the truth of an A proposition, one can infer the falsity of its contradictory, the O proposition. Alternatively, if the A is false, then the O is true. Similar valid inferences occur between the contradictories E and I. These relationships are displayed in the following chart.

Chart 3.3: Immediate Inferences

	A is	E is	I is	O is
If A be true	true	false	true	false
If E be true	false	true	false	true
If I be true	**	false	true	**
If O be true	false	**	**	true

(** Truth-Value is undetermined – always in pairs.)

To demonstrate the relationship between the Square of Opposition and the Clark Diagram in a manner that applies the definition of valid inference as a rule or test of validity, consider once again a previously cited implication: "Is A(ab) implies I(ab) a valid inference?"

The Square of Opposition displays the relation of subalternation between an A Form and an I Form. Thus, A(ab) implies I(ab), by this account, is a valid inference. Suppose now someone requests a more convincing demonstration and asks: Is the form of the conclusion (Some a is b) true every time the form of the premise (All a is b) is?

The Clark Diagram of five sets of circles provides the answer. I(ab), *Some a is b*, is true every time A(ab), *All a is b*, is true. I(ab) is true in Cases 1-4, the first four diagrams; A(ab) is true in the first two of the four. Thus the form of the conclusion is true every time(1-4) the form of the premise is true (1-2). Therefore, A(ab) implies I(ab) is a valid inference by the application of the valid inference definition.

Additional evidence confirming the validity of the inference can be seen in Lines I and A. *Line I* includes *Line A* just as the first four diagrams include the first two.

Square of Opposition Inferences

Before we list the immediate inferences depicted by the Square of Opposition, two observations are in order.

First, note that the *not* attached to a form below means the form is *false*; otherwise, *true*. (In every question that follows, assume that a form is true, unless it is designated false by the prefix "not".)

Second, we formulate immediate inferences as *logical* implications in accord with the logic of necessary inference. (Grammatically, one must understand the distinction in usage between "infer" versus "imply." Thus, *to imply* may mean *to state indirectly*, and *to infer* may mean *to deduce a statement or a conclusion*. In our use, *logical implication* is but another way of expressing necessary implication or inference.)

For example, one could ask: Is I(ab) a necessary consequence of A(ab)? That is to say: Does A(ab) logically imply I(ab)? Below, we list which of the four forms is logically implied by each.

Immediate Inferences (1-4)

Form A(ab): 1a to 1d Questions and Answers

Question 1a: Does A(ab) logically imply I(ab)?

- Answer 1a: Yes, by Subalternation.

- Example 1a: if it is true that "All men are mortal," then "Some men are mortal" is true.

Question 1b: Does A(ab) logically imply not-E(ab)?

- Answer 1b: Yes, by Contraries.

- Example 1b: From the truth of "All men are sinners," one can state as a necessary consequence that it is false that "No man is a sinner."

Question 1c: Does A(ab) logically imply not-O(ab)?

- Answer 1c: Yes, by Contradiction.

- Example 1c: From the true "All men are mortal" the contradictory, "Some men are not mortal" is false.

Question 1d: Does *not*-A(ab) logically imply O(ab)?

- Answer 1d: Yes by Contradiction.

- Example 1d: From the false "All men are saved," the contradictory, "Some men are not saved," is true.

Form E(ab): 2a to 2d Questions and Answers

Question 2a: Does E(ab) logically imply O(ab)?

- Answer 2a: Yes by Subalternation.

- Example 2a: If it is true that "No hater-of-logic is a lover-of-truth," then the corresponding O form is also true.

Question 2b: Does E(ab) logically imply *not*-A(ab)?

- Answer 2b: Yes by Contraries.

- Example 2b: If it is true that "No man is saved by his own efforts," then it is false that "All men are saved by their own efforts."

Question 2c: Does E(ab) logically imply *not*-I(ab)?

- Answer 2c: Yes by Contradiction.

- Example 2c: If "No man is saved by his own efforts" is true, then it is false that "Some are so saved."

Question 2d: Does *not*-E(ab) logically imply I(ab)?

- Answer 2d: Yes by Contradiction.

- Example 2d: If it is false that "No men are saved," then the contradictory, "Some men are saved," is true.

Form I(ab): 3a to 3d Questions and Answers

Question 3a: Does I(ab) logically imply *not*-E(ab)?

- Answer 3a: Yes by Contradiction.

- Example 3a: If it is true that "Some persons are Christian," then it is false that "No persons are Christian."

Question 3b: Does *not*-I(ab) logically imply E(ab)?

- Answer 3b: Yes by Contradiction.

- Example 3b: If it is false that "Some sinners are saved by their own efforts," then the contradictory is true: "No sinners are saved by their own efforts."

Question 3c: Does *not*-I(ab) logically imply O(ab)?

- Answer 3c: Yes by Subcontraries.

- Example 3c: If it is false that "Some sinners are saved by their own efforts," then it is true that "Some sinners are not saved by their own efforts."

Question 3d: Does *not*-I(ab) logically imply *not*-A(ab)?

- Answer 3d: Yes by Subalternation.

- Example 3d: If it is false that "Some sinners are saved by their own efforts," then, it is false that "All are so saved." (Note the cells in Chart 3.3 where the truth-value is undetermined.)

Form O(ab): 4a to 4d Questions and Answers

Question 4a: Does O(ab) logically imply *not*-A(ab)?

- Answer 4a: Yes by Contradiction.

- Example 4a: If it is true that "Some persons are not Christian," then it is false that "All persons are Christian."

Question 4b: Does *not*-O(ab) logically imply A(ab)?

- Answer 4b: Yes by Contradiction.

- Example 4b: If it is false that "Some persons are not mortal," then the contradictory is true: "All persons are mortal."

Question 4c: Does *not*-O(ab) logically imply I(ab)?

- Answer 4c: Yes by Subcontraries.

- Example 4c: If it is false that "Some persons are not mortal," then it is true that "Some persons are mortal."

Question 4d: Does *not*-O(ab) logically imply not-E(ab)?

29

- Answer 4d: Yes by Subalternation.

- Example 4d: If it is false that "Some persons are not mortal," then it is false that "No persons are mortal." (However, from the truth of the O-Form, the truth-value of the E-Form is undetermined. See Chart 3.3.)

Repetition does have benefits. Test each of the sixteen inferences for validity by using the circles and lines of Chart 3.1. The student will not only gain practice using the diagrams and lines of the chart but also acquire skill for determining the validity or invalidity of inferences.

For example, assuming A(ab) is true, what can be said about the truth-value (truth or falsity) of E(ab)?

The lines (on the Chart) A and E do not overlap. What does this mean? Answer: Whenever this condition holds, it means, A and E cannot both be true together. Thus, if A(ab), *All a is b is true*, the circles of Cases 1 and 2, then E(ab), *No a is b*, is false, that is, the circles of Case 5 do not obtain.

Invalid Inferences

We have shown the value of Chart 3.1 in testing the validity of the immediate inferences depicted in the Square of Opposition. Obviously, use of the same method proves invalidity as well, for if a logical implication is not valid, then it must be invalid -- the only other possibility.

Consider the list of expressions in Table 3.1 that follows. This table shows the number of ways two forms can be combined to form implications. The purpose here is to make use of our charts, in particular Chart 3.1.

Using "<" for "logically implies" which of the inferences in Tables 3.1 and 3.2 are shown to be invalid and which are shown to be valid?

For example, the first implication in Table 3.1 First Figure is A(ab) < E(ab). It may be read as the question, "Does A(ab) logically imply E(ab)?"

Answer: No, invalid because E(ab) is not true every time A(ab) is true; E(ab) is true once in the fifth Case; A(ab) is true twice in Cases 1 and 2.

Another example: the last implication in Table 3.1, O(ab) < I(ab), is invalid, since I(ab) is true four times (Cases 1, 2, 3, and 4), while O(ab) is true three times (Cases 3, 4, and 5).

The form of the conclusion must be true every time the form of the premise is true.

Practice using Chart 3.1 is essential; therefore, 1.2 through 1.7 should receive similar treatment as has been shown with the first and last.

Table 3.1: First Figure

1.1. Does A(ab) < E(ab)?	1.5. Does I(ab) < A(ab)?
1.2. Does A(ab) < I(ab)?	1.6. Does I(ab) < O(ab)?
1.3. Does E(ab) < A(ab)?	1.7. Does O(ab) < E(ab)?
1.4. Does E(ab) < O(ab)?	1.8. Does O(ab) < I(ab)?

The list of implications above (1.1-1.8) are in the First Figure. A difference in figure means a difference in the order of terms of the consequent of the implication, such that reordering the terms of the conclusion produces another set of implications, said to be in the Second Figure. For example: A(ab) is in the First Figure; A(ba) is in the Second Figure. (Or if A(ba) is considered to be in the First Figure, then A(ab) is in the Second Figure.) There are only two figures for immediate inferences.

Sufficient information has been provided for the student to do an exercise: show which of the implications in the Second Figure that follow are invalid. (Remember that the order of the terms of the conclusions of 2.1-2.8 in Table 3.2 have been reversed.)

Table 3.2: Second Figure

2.1. Does A(ab) < E(ba)?	2.5. Does I(ab) < A(ba)?
2.2. Does A(ab) < I(ba)?	2.6. Does I(ab) < O(ba)?
2.3. Does E(ab) < A(ba)?	2.7. Does O(ab) < E(ba)?
2.4. Does E(ab) < O(ba)?	2.8. Does O(ab) < I(ba)?

Other Immediate Inferences

Three other immediate inferences for the four forms are conversion, obversion, and contraposition. Definitions with commentary follow in the order listed.

Conversion (5-7)

The converse of a proposition is formed by interchanging the subject and predicate. For example, the converse of "Some men are believers." is "Some believers are men." Application of conversion yields the following:

5. I(ab) logically implies I(ba). Chart 3.1 shows that every time I(ba) is true, so is I(ab)

6. E(ab) logically implies E(ba). Every time E(ba) is true, so is E(ab), as the Chart 3.1 shows.

7. A(ab) logically implies I(ba). This implication is valid only by *conversion per accidens*, from "All" to "Some". Chart 3.1 shows: I(ab) is true every time A(ab) is true. Then by conversion, *I(ab) < I(ba)* is valid.

The O form has no converse, since to permit it warrants drawing a false proposition from a true one. For example, the converse of the true proposition "Some vegetables are not carrots" would be the false proposition "Some carrots are not vegetables." Moreover, O(ba) is not true every time O(ab) is true; check Chart 3.1 diagrams again. (Note as well that *O(ab) < O(ba)* is invalid, since a term in the premise which is undistributed, is distributed in the conclusion.)

Obversion (8-11)

To form the obverse of a proposition, change the quality of the proposition and replace the predicate by its complement. For example, the obverse of "All believers are saved" is "No believers are non-saved." A term and its complement are said to exhaust the universe of objects. Thus, if "S" stands for the class *Saved*, "S' " (read: *S-prime* or *non-S*) stands for the complement class, *non-Saved*. The combined classes *SS'* totally exhaust the universe of entities, since everything in the universe must fall either into one class or its complement class. Each of the four forms has an obverse.

8. A(ab) logically implies E(ab'), the obverse. In other words, *All a is b* logically implies *No a is non-b.*. Thus, if All men are sinners, then No men

are non-sinners.

9. E(ab) logically implies A(ab'), the obverse. Or, *No a is b* logically implies *All a is non-b*. If No atheists are Christian, then All atheists are non-Christian.

10. I(ab) logically implies O(ab'), the obverse. Rephrasing: *Some a is b* logically implies *Some a is not non-b*. Thus, if Some men are efficient, then Some men are not inefficient (non-efficient).

11. O(ab) logically implies I(ab'), the obverse. Rewording: *Some a is not b* logically implies *Some a is non-b*. Thus, if some things are not excusable, then some things are inexcusable (non-excusable).

Contraposition (12-14)

The contrapositive of a proposition is one in which the complement terms of the subject and predicate are interchanged. Contraposition of a form obtains by first obverting the original, converting the resulting proposition, then obverting once again. For example, the proposition "All humans are mortal" obverts to "No humans are immortal (non-mortal)" which converts to "No non-mortal persons are human" which when obverted yields "All non-mortals are non-human."

12. A(ab) logically implies A(b'a'), the contrapositive. Reread the example as shown above. Note: the contrapositive of A(b'a') is A(ab).

13. E(ab) logically implies O(b'a'), the contrapositive. The obverse of an E form yields an A form which when converted yields an I form. (Recall, the A form undergoes *conversion per accidens*, or conversion by limitation of quantity from universal to particular.) Obverting this I form results in the contrapositive O form.

Example: If "No ungraciousness is excusable behavior," then it follows that "Some inexcusable behavior is not gracious."

The step by step process is shown below.

Form E: "No ungraciousness is excusable."

Step 1: Obversion: "All ungraciousness is inexcusable." (Changed Quality from Negative to Affirmative and predicate replaced by complement.)

Step 2: Conversion by Limitation: "Some inexcusable behavior is ungracious." (Changed Quantity from Universal to Particular; terms are exchanged.)

Step 3: Obversion: "Some inexcusable behavior is not gracious." (Changed quality, replaced predicate as in Step 1 above.)

14. O(ab) logically implies O(b'a'), the contrapositive. Some a is not b logically implies Some non-b is not non-a.

Consider: Some pleasant things are not worthy. Does this mean that some unworthy things are not unpleasant? Answer: Yes.

The I form has no contrapositive since to permit it would warrant drawing a false proposition from a true one. For example, *Some human beings are irreverent*, but does that mean that *Some reverent persons are non-human?* Obviously not. Performing a step-by-step contraposition of the I form (Obversion, Conversion, then Obversion), it obverts to an O form, but since the O form has no converse, the process of contraposition is aborted.

Chart 3.4 summarizes these three immediate inferences. Each immediate inference has its original in the Form column.

Chart 3.4: Summary of Three Immediate Inferences

Form	Conversion	Obversion	Contraposition
A(ab)	I(ba)*	E(ab')	A(b'a')
E(ab)	E(ba)	A(ab')	O(b'a')
I(ab)	I(ba)	O(ab')	(None)
O(ab)	(None)	I(ab')	O(b'a')

*Conversion per accidens (by limitation)

Review: We have suggested that immediate inferences can be more properly treated as logical implications. We introduced the symbol "<" to stand for *logically implies*, and the prime symbol " ' " to designate the complement of the form to which it is attached.

Conversion is simple enough being the exchange of the terms of the E and I forms. There is no converse for the O form, and the A form converts by limitation.

Two previous examples are cited below for review: one for obversion, the other for contraposition.

Obversion #8:

A(ab)<E(ab′) is a valid logical implication. The conclusion is obtained by obverting the premise, A(ab) in this manner: change the quality of the A form from affirmative to negative and replace its predicate (b) by its complement, (b′).

Contraposition #14:

O(ab)<O(b′a′) is a valid logical implication. The conclusion is obtained by interchanging the complements of the terms in the premise, O(ab). Or, using the step-by-step procedure, we obvert, then convert, then obvert as described in what follows: Premise: O(ab).

Step 1. obvert above to I(ab′)

Step 2. convert I(ab′) to I(b′a)

Step 3. obvert I(b′a) to O(b′a′)

The formulation of immediate inferences as logical implications using the "<" and " ′ " as required, and applying Chart 3.1 features to determine validity, is a procedure which becomes complicated and tiresome for obversion and contraposition. For these reasons, we have evaluated these immediate inferences using definitions. Nevertheless, all of the immediate inferences can be tested using Chart 3.1. Should the student be inclined to carry out this process, it should be noted that for each case, everything outside of circle *a* is *a′* (non-a),everything outside of circle *b* is *b′* (non-b), and vice versa. These additional notations must be filled in the 5 Cases of circles correctly for accurate results.

Three Additional Inferences (15-17)

The remaining immediate inferences are three: reflexive, symmetrical, and transitive. These inferences apply to relationships, like "is greater than," or "is less than," when speaking of numbers or quantities. One or more may apply to other types of relationships; for example, family relationships, "the son of" or "the sister of," and so forth. Some relationships exhibit one or more; some none.

15. Reflexive

The reflexive relationship is a relation in which each element is in relation to itself. Equality in arithmetic is reflexive: *five* equals *five*, *ten* equals *ten*, and so forth. Implication in logic is reflexive; each proposition implies itself.

16. Symmetrical

Symmetrical relationships are those which hold for *a and b*, and also for *b and a*. If a is the cousin of b, does it follow that b is the cousin of a? Obviously. However, do you see that symmetry is not present if *a is the sister of b?* (Assume *b* is male.) What can be said of "is the twin of?" Is it symmetrical? Logical Implication is not symmetrical, with the exception of the Law of Identity – every proposition implies itself.

17. Transitive

Transitive relationships are a bit more complicated to explain but easier to illustrate. The relationships "is less than," "is greater than," "is subsequent to," "is parallel to," link together three terms in a unique fashion. If *a is greater than b*, and *b is greater than c*, then it follows necessarily that *a is greater than c.* The relationship "is the brother of" is not transitive. Logical implication is transitive: *if a logically implies b, and b logically implies c, then a logically implies c.* The basic principle may be understood thus: a relation is transitive when it holds for *a and b*, and it also holds for *b and c*, then it thereby holds between *a and c.*

Summary

As has been shown, knowledge of the definitions of immediate inferences when applied correctly will distinguish valid from invalid inferences. We summarize with an example:

What valid inferences (necessary consequences) follow from "There is therefore now no condemnation to them which are in Christ Jesus, who walk not after the flesh, but after the Spirit," reworded so that the sense of the A form is clear?

Using the parameter "persons," yields this:

All persons-who-are-in-Christ Jesus-who-walk-not-after-the-flesh-but-after-the-Spirit are persons-for-whom-there-is-now-no-condemnation.

The related I form is true by subalternation; the E form is false by contraries; the contradictory O form is false.

The wealth of immediate inferences available from a set of four standard form propositions is extensive. We turn in the next chapter to the syllogism.

Review

1. List all of the valid immediate inferences that follow from the Biblical passage cited in the summary section of this chapter.

2. Why is it invalid to infer from *All a is b*, that *All b is a*? Does Chart 3.1, Case 1 of circles show this inference to be valid?

3. Why is the distribution of terms a matter of importance for immediate inference arguments? Do the circles of Chart 3.1 incorporate or otherwise include the characteristic of distribution for the terms of the forms?

4. If you have not memorized the definition of valid inference, take time to do so now. *If the Form of a conclusion is true every time the Forms of the premises are true, the argument is valid.* (Incidentally, in logic, why do not we speak of "a true argument," or "a valid statement?")

5. If someone asserts, "Some politicians are liars." and another, disagreeing, says, "Some politicians are not liars." are they contradicting each other?

Exercise 3.1 Immediate Inferences

Instructions: Choose the letter of the most correct answer for each statement. For any instance of " j " (None of the Above) provide the correct answer.

a	contradiction	f	obversion
b	contraposition	g	subcontraries
c	contraries	h	subalterns
d	conversion	i	valid
e	invalid	j	None of the Above

	STATEMENTS	
1	The forms A(ab) and E(ab) are opposed as _____, meaning they cannot be true together but may both be false.	
2	The forms I and O are opposed as _____, meaning they cannot both be false but may both be true.	
3	The forms A(ab) and I(ab) can both be true or both be false meaning they are _____.	
4	The relationship between the forms E and I is called _____.	
5	If from form E(ab), we conclude E(ba), the inference is called _____.	
6	_____ for the form O(ab) is not valid.	
7	The form A(ab) implies A(b′ a′) by _____.	
8	The form A(ab) implies E(ab′) by _____.	
9	The inference A(ab) < A(ba) is _____.	
10	The inference E(ab) < O(b′a′) is _____.	
11	The inference A(ab) < I(ba) is _____.	
12	The inference I(ab) < I(b′ a′) is _____.	
13	The strongest opposition between two forms is _____.	
14	The _____ E(ab) and O(ab) are both false when A(ab) is true.	
15	_____ is valid for each of the four forms.	

Exercise 3.2: Validity of Immediate Inferences

Instructions: Use the Clark Diagram. For each Item determine the validity or invalidity of the implication. Mark V for valid; I for invalid.

	STATEMENTS	V or I
1	A(ab) logically implies E(ab′).	

2	A(ab) logically implies I(ab).	
3	A(ab) logically implies O(ab).	
4	E(ab) logically implies A(ab').	
5	E(ab) logically implies I(a'b).	
6	E(ab) logically implies O(ab).	
7	I(ab) logically implies I(ba).	
8	I(ab) logically implies I(b'a').	
9	I(ab) logically implies O(ab').	
10	O(ab) logically implies A(ab').	
11	O(ab) logically implies O(b'a').	
12	O(ab) logically implies I(ab').	

Exercise 3.3: Additional Immediate Inferences

Instructions: Which of the following is true and which is false?

	STATEMENTS	T / F
1	A symmetrical relationship is one that holds between one of it objects and the object itself.	
2	2=2 in arithmetic is reflexive.	
3	The reflexive relationship is one which holds for *a and b*, and also *b and a*.	
4	"X is the cousin of Y" is a symmetrical relationship	
5	" is less than," and "is greater than" are transitive relationships.	
6	Logical implication is not transitive.	
7	"is the ancestor of" is a transitive relationship	

4 THE SYLLOGISM

While immediate inference contained two propositions, a premise and a conclusion, and thus, two and only two terms, a standard syllogism contains more. The familiar syllogism of men, mortals, and Socrates will again prove its value, providing the basis for introducing new terms and new definitions. The "∴" is read as "therefore."

All men are mortal.

Socrates is a man.

∴ Socrates is mortal.

The Basic Elements

The propositions of a standard syllogism must be standard form propositions. A standard syllogism must contain three and only three propositions, two of which are premises; the other is the conclusion. The two premises and the conclusion share three and only three terms. Each term appears twice, but never twice in the same proposition.

In the syllogism above, the three terms are *men, mortal,* and *Socrates.* Each one appears twice: *Socrates* in the conclusion and the second premise; *mortal* in the conclusion and the first premise; and *men (or man)* in the two premises. Each term not only appears twice, but must mean the same thing each time. When the two instances of a term mean the same thing, then the term is *univocal* in meaning. For example, "mortal" in the conclusion and the premise must be univocal. Thus, a syllogism is an argument having two premises and a conclusion with the subject term of the conclusion in one of the premises, the conclusion's predicate term in the other premise, and a third term in both premises. The third term of the premises must never appear in the conclusion. An examination of the syllogism above meets all of the requirements of a standard syllogism.

The Terms of the Syllogism

The syllogism above can be expressed as a logical implication:

$$A(ba) \ A(cb) < A(ca)$$

where *a* stands for mortal; *b* stands for man; *c* stands for Socrates; and "<" stands for logically implies. The letter *A* designates A-Form propositions.

The implication above can be expressed as an argument.

Major Premise	A(ba)
Minor Premise	A(cb)
Conclusion	∴ A(ca)

The subject term of the conclusion is the minor term (c). The predicate of the conclusion is the major term (a). The term that appears in both premises, but not the conclusion, is the middle term (b). The premise that contains the major term is the major premise and is first. The premise that contains the minor term is the minor premise and is second after the major premise.

Thus, the conclusion of our syllogism is an inference from the major premise through the *mediation* of the minor premise.

The Mood of a Syllogism

The *mood* of an argument is an individual case of an inference. For example, each of the propositions of the syllogism above are of the form *All a is b* -- the *A Form*. The *mood*, we say, is *AAA*; the first letter denotes the form of the first premise, the second letter denotes the form of the second premise, and the third letter denotes the form of the conclusion. Thus, the *mood* refers to the forms of the propositions of the syllogism and their order, beginning with the major and ending with the conclusion. Every standard syllogism has a mood of three and only three forms.

The Figure of a Syllogism

The *figure* of a syllogism means the relative locations of the term shared only by the premises, the middle term. Omitting for this purpose any reference to the conclusions, the four figures of any syllogism are shown below. It may be helpful to think of Figures 1 and 4 as mirror images of each other, as are Figures 2 and 3.

In the following table, *s* stands for the minor term; *m* stands for the middle term; and *p* stands for the major term.

Major Premise	M-p	p-M	M-p	p-M
Minor Premise	s-M	s-M	M-s	M-s
Figure	1	2	3	4

By figure, then, we indicate the relative positions of the one term shared by both premises -- the middle term.

The Frame of a Syllogism

The *frame* of a syllogism is the combination its mood and figure. Thus, when we speak of the form of a syllogism, we mean the frame -- its mood and figure together. Our syllogism above has this frame: AAA-1.

Valid syllogistic frames have been given names by logicians. In part, their purpose was the development of a system of frame-names in verses as a memory device to aid in identifying the different valid moods and figures of the syllogism. Additional characteristics incorporated in these names are described in due course.

Four propositional forms can be combined in pairs resulting in 16 different sets of premises: A-A, A-E, A-I, A-O; E-E, E-A, E-O, E-I; etc. Since each pair may have any one of the four forms as a conclusion, the number of moods is 16 x 4, or 64. There are 4 figures that factor in the total; thus 64 x 4 results in a total of 256 frames. Not all of these frames received names, only the valid ones. There are 24 valid frames, hardly as intimidating as 256, if one had to rely on memory. Fortunately, there are rules, subsequently described, that simplify the task of determining the validity of any frame.

Syllogism Validity

As stated, *valid* is a quality of arguments in which the claim of logical necessity for the conclusion is established. Recall, an argument is valid if the form of the conclusion is true every time the forms of the premises are true.

The application of rules or the method of deduction, subsequently discussed, determine the validity or invalidity of a standard syllogism.

We start with rules since they are easy to apply once we make explicit an argument's frame .The valid frames are the source of the rules themselves. There are five rules that taken as axioms provide an alternative to the deductive method for proving valid frames as theorems. Still, the beginning student should be acquainted with the method of deduction. To that end, following the discussion of the five rules, we prove as theorems seven of the 24 valid frames. These should suffice to introduce a beginner to the significance of the deductive method in syllogistic reasoning. The use of diagrams, to show rather than prove validity or invalidity, are described using selected argument forms to introduce beginning students to this technique.

Five Rules

1 Two premises in both of which the middle term is
   undistributed do not logically imply a conclusion.
2 Two premises with undistributed terms having a conclusion

that distributes those same terms do not logically imply a conclusion.

3   Two affirmative premises do not logically imply a negative conclusion.

4   Two negative premises do not logically imply a conclusion.

5   An affirmative and negative pair of premises does not logically imply an affirmative conclusion.

A syllogism is valid when it satisfies all of the rules. The syllogism at the beginning of the chapter is valid by each of these rules. The rules are both *sufficient* and *necessary*. They are *sufficient* in that their application confirms the validity the 24 syllogisms proved valid by the deductive method and prove the remaining ones invalid. The rules are also *necessary* since each rule applies to at least one invalid syllogism for which none of the others apply.

A study of the rules alone will eliminate a number of invalid frames. For example, by Rule 4, the syllogisms with premises E-E, E-O, O-O, and O-E (all negative) are invalid. Rule 1 declares invalid the syllogisms with premises I-I, O-I, figures 1 & 3 and I-O, figures 3 & 4, since these combinations leave the middle term undistributed. Indeed, a systematic study of the rules should eliminate as invalid all but 24 of the 256 frames. This is the significance of *necessary* and *sufficient* rules.

The Method of Deduction

It is an unavoidable fact that every system of thought, philosophy, theology, or body of knowledge has starting points without which the system could not get off the ground. To put it another way: every system of thought or knowledge has an axiom or a set of axioms that are indemonstrable within that system. An *axiom* is a first principle or premise that cannot be demonstrated precisely because axioms themselves are used to demonstrate or prove other statements known as *theorems*. A *theorem* is a deduction from an axiom. Theorems may also be deductions from a combination of axioms and theorems previously deduced from axioms. In short, theorems are propositions deduced from axioms or first principles. First principles, axioms, are the basis of all argument and demonstration.

Following Clark, we shall use axioms, two principles or decision rules, and some definitions to deduce seven valid syllogisms as theorems. (Note that the following axioms expressed as frames, AAA-1 and EAE-1 are valid by the five rules for testing the validity of argument forms.)

Axiom 1 A(ba) A(cb) < A(ca)

Axiom 2 E(ba) A(cb) < E(ca)

Two principles (decision rules) applied to the above axioms to deduce theorems, or to deduce additional theorems from previous deductions, follow.

Principle 1

A valid inference results if in any valid implication the premise and the conclusion are interchanged and contradicted.

For example, A(ab) < I(ab) is a valid inference. Application of this principle to the valid inference yields: E(ab) < O(ab), a valid inference.

Principle 2

In any valid implication, if its premise be *strengthened* or its conclusion be *weakened*, a valid implication will result.

For example, E(ab) < E(ba) is a valid implication where the conclusion is a weakened form of the premise. Note: Conversion of the E and I forms and the A form by limitation are part of the denotation of Principle 2.

To illustrate, we know that A(ab)<I(ab) is a valid implication by subalternation. In this implication, A(ab) can be said to be a *strengthened form* of I(ab), and I(ab) is a *weakened form* of A(ab). Of course, one can also deduce A(ab) < I(ab) as a theorem, from A(ab) < A(ab), the latter being valid by the law of identity. The conclusion A(ab) has been replaced by its *weakened* form, I(ab) in Step 1 below.

An additional theorem is deduced in Step 2 by applying Principle 1 to the theorem of Step 1.

(Ax for Axiom, Th for theorem, and Pr for Principle)

A(ab) < A(ab) Law of Identity -- Ax

Step1 A(ab) < I(ab) Th#1, by Pr 2, replacing the conclusion of the Axiom in Step 1 by its weakened form, I(ab).

Step2   E(ab) < O(ab)   Th #2, by Pr 1, interchanging and contradicting the premise and conclusion of Th #1.

We undertake now the deduction of the first four of seven theorems from two axioms and the use of the two principles described above.

Deduction of Theorems (1-4)

	A(ba) A(cb) < A(ca)	Ax 1
	E(ba) A(cb) < E(ca)	Ax 2
Step1	A(ba) O(ca) < O(cb)	Th #1, by Pr 1 (interchange minor premise & conclusion of Ax 1 & contradict)
Step2	O(ca) A(cb) < O(ba)	Th #2, by Pr 1 (interchange major premise & conclusion of Ax 1 & contradict)
Step3	I(ca) A(cb) < I(ba)	Th #3, by Pr 1 (interchange major premise & conclusion of Ax 2 & contradict)
Step4	E(ba) I(ca) < O(cb)	Th #4, by Pr 1 (interchange minor premise & conclusion of Ax 2 & contradict)

Changing a theorem's terms to achieve a uniform or consistent format is required for classification as valid moods/figures or frame names. Theorems 1-4 above are not in Conventional Form. Axioms 1 and 2 above are in Conventional Form. So, let us stipulate that "a" is the major term, "b" is the middle term, and "c" is the minor term. Applying these conventions to Theorems 1-4, we obtain the Conventional Forms and thereby the correct mood and figure.

Conventional Forms of Theorems

Theorems	Conventional Form	Frame
1 A(ba) O(ca) < O(cb)	A(ab) O(cb) < O(ca)	AOO-2
2 O(ca) A(cb) < O(ba)	O(ba) A(bc) < O(ca)	OAO-3
3 I(ca) A(cb) < I(ba)	I(ba) A(bc) < I(ca)	IAI-3

4 E(ba) I(ca) < O(cb)	E(ab) I(cb) < O(ca)	EIO-2

Theorems 1-4 may now be used together with the original axioms and principles (1 & 2) to prove the remaining three of the seven valid syllogisms as theorems.

(Note: In addition to abbreviations for axiom, theorem, and principle, three other abbreviations are used below: wfc = weakened form of conclusion, sfp = strengthened form of premise, and CF = conventional form.)

Deduction of Theorems (5-7)

	A(ba) A(cb) < A(ca)	Ax 1
	E(ba) A(cb) < E(ca)	Ax 2
Step5	E(ba) A(cb) < E(ac)	Th 5, by Prin 2, wfc Ax 2 (conversion of conclusion*)
Step6	E(ba) A(cb) < O(ca)	Th 6, by Prin 2 wfc on Ax 2
Step7	E(ba) A(cb) < O(ac)	Th 7, by Prin 2 wfc on Th5*

*Not in Conventional Form

Our reasoning falls along these lines: in Step5, E(ca) < E(ac) is a valid conversion of an E proposition. The conclusions of our two axioms and Theorem 5 are universal in quantity. A universal conclusion validly implies its corresponding particular. In other words:

In Step 5, E(ac) is a weakened form of the conclusion, E(ca) of Axiom 2;

In Step 6, O(ca) is a weakened form of the conclusion, E(ca) of Axiom 2; and

In Step 7, O(ac) is a weakened form of the conclusion, E(ac) of Theorem 5.

Theorem 6 is in conventional form. Theorems 5 and 7 are not. With Theorems 5 and 7, the conventional form will also require a re-ordering of the premises. Recall that the premise with the major term (the same as the predicate term of the conclusion) is the major premise and is placed first. The minor premise, the premise with the minor term, (the same as the subject term of the conclusion) is second. (Also recall that "a" is the major term; "b" is the middle term; and "c" is the minor term.)

Th	Deduction	CF	Frame
5	E(ba) A(cb) < E(ac)	A(ab) E(bc) < E(ca)	AEE-4
6*	E(ba) A(cb) < O(ca)*	E(ba) A(cb) < O(ca)	EAO-1
7	E(ba) A(cb) < O(ac)	A(ab) E(bc) < O(ca)	AEO-4

*Already in Conventional Form (CF)

At this point, the deductive method has proven 7 theorems from 2 axioms, using the principles and definitions provided. Careful application of the deductive method will result in valid deductions of the remaining fifteen frames -- a challenge for the student to complete. (Note: There are 24 valid frames, 2 of which were used as axioms. Adding the 7 already deduced, brings the number to 9. Subtracting 9 from 24 valid frames, leaves 15 remaining to be deduced.) If you deduce one that is doubtful, appeal to the 5 rules to check your deductive reasoning.

Frame Names

As mentioned previously, the valid frames of syllogistic logic were given names with key letters; the vowels indicate the mood. Other lower case letters stand for certain operations we shall describe subsequently. The nineteen names designate nineteen frames. Five other frames may be added on the basis already mentioned; namely, that the universal conclusion of a valid frame implies the corresponding particular. For example, from Axiom 1, Barbara or AAA-1, one can deduce the theorem having this mood and figure: AAI-1. The AAI-1 frame is the *Weakened Form of Barbara*. Similarly, from Axiom 2, Celarent or EAE-1, one can deduce a theorem having this mood and figure: EAO-1. The EAO-1 frame is the *Weakened Form of Celarent*.

Figures and Names of 19 Valid Syllogisms

1st Figure	2nd Figure	3rd Figure	4th Figure
Barbara (AAA)	Cesare (EAE)	Darapti (AAI)	Bramantip (AAI)
Celarent (EAE)	Camestres (AEE)	Disamis (IAI)	Camenes (AEE)

Darii (AII)	Festino (EIO)	Datisi (AII)	Dimaris (IAI)
Ferio (EIO)	Baroko (AOO)	Felapton (EAO)	Fesapo (EAO)
		Bokardo (OAO)	Fresison (EIO)
		Ferison (EIO)	
1st Figure	2nd Figure	3rd Figure	4th Figure

The names of Theorems 1-7 already deduced. See Chart 4.1. (*Note: "wf" = weakened form.)

Chart 4.1: Theorems and Frame Names

CF Theorems (1-7)		Frames	Names
1	A(ab) O(cb) < O(ca)	AOO-2	Baroko
2	O(ba) A(bc) < O(ca)	OAO-3	Bokardo
3	I(ba) A(bc) < I(ca)	IAI-3	Disamis
4	E(ab) I(cb) < O(ca)	EIO-2	Festino
5	A(ab) E(bc) < E(ca)	AEE-4	Camenes
6	E(ba) A(cb) < O(ca)	EAO-1	Celarent-1, wf*
7	A(ab) E(bc) < O(ca)	AEO-4	Camenes-4, wf *

Examine the names. The vowels of the names, as mentioned above, stand for the mood of the syllogism. The other letters of the first figure names do not have any special meaning, but the "s," "p," "m," and "k" of the other figures (2, 3, and 4) do have special meanings as described in what follows.

"s" stands for simple conversion of the preceding proposition. For example, if in Camenes you convert the conclusion E(ca) to E(ac) and change to conventional form, which in this case requires a reordering of the premises, you deduce Celarent, EAE-1.

"p" means to convert the preceding proposition by limitation or *per accidens*. If you apply this operation to Fesapo (EAO-4), you get Festino (EIO-2).

"m" means to change the order of the premises so that the major premise is first to achieve the conventional form of the syllogism.

"k" stands for *reductio ad absurdum* (RAA), or assuming the conclusion to be false as part of the premise set in order to deduce by valid inferences, step by step, a contradiction. In this manner, one demonstrates that the assumption of a false conclusion as premise was unwarranted, and the original implication, therefore valid. To illustrate, let us show that Bokardo (OAO-3) is valid by RAA proof.

$$O(ba) \ A(bc) \therefore O(ca) \ \text{Bokardo-3}$$

1.	O(ba)	true premise	$\therefore$ O(ca)
2.	A(bc)	true premise	
Assume	3. O(ca) is false	RAA method	
Then	4. A(ca) is true	Contradictory of 3	
Then	5. A(ca) A(bc)<A(ba)	4 & 2 Barbara-1	
But	6. A(ba) can't be true	Contradictory of 1, O(ba)	
So	7. A(ba) must be false	$\therefore$1 & 6 contradictory	
But if	8. A(ba) is false	Step 7	
Then	9. A(ca) or A(bc) is false	5 (Barbara-1) & 8	
Option1 Assume	10. A(ca) is false	From Step 9	
Then	11. O(ca), 3 can't be false	3 & 10 contradictory	
Then	12. O(ca) is both true & false	3 & 11 Impossible!	

Option2 Assume	13. A(bc) is false	From Step 9
Then	14. A(bc) is both true & false	2 & 13 Impossible!
∴	15. O(ba) A(bc) < O(ca)	Valid Bokardo

Step 15: In assuming the true premises of OAO-3 in conjunction with a denial of its conclusion, the deductive method has led, by valid inferences, to contradictions in Steps 12 and 14. Therefore, the conclusion O(ca) must be True and Bokardo-3 is a valid frame.

Venn Diagrams

Recall the definition for valid inference. A valid inference from premises to conclusions depends on the arrangement of the subject and predicate being true in the conclusion, every time the arrangement of the same subject and predicate is true in the premises.

The use of circles, invented by the mathematician, Euler, can show how an inference is valid or invalid. Of course, the method using Euler Circles (or Venn Diagrams) is perhaps not the best way for showing validity. Two reasons come to mind. First, there is the suspicious assumption about the logical properties of classes coinciding precisely with the properties of circles. Second, the drawing of circles, the number required, the correct configurations, and learning what to see, can be complicated. Besides, it is so much easier to memorize five rules, and developing skills in their application follows nicely. Nevertheless, the student of logic should not be ignorant of all available methods. Hence, this section will describe procedures for the use of Euler Circles (Venn Diagrams) and illustrate their application.

Step 1: Start with the major premise. The required number of complete sets of diagrams for the major premise will depend on the required number of individual diagrams for the minor. Chart 3.1 will show you the number required for each form: the A requires two, the E requires 1, and so forth.

Step 2: Next, impose (or map) each set of the minor premise on a set of the major premise.

Step 3: Then, examine the circles to determine whether or not the resultant diagrams include the form of the conclusion–every time. If the answer is "yes," the syllogism is valid; otherwise, invalid.

(Note: In the following diagrams, capitalization of variables for ease of identification.)

Now, to display applications using Frame: AOI-2

Major Premise	All cats are felines.	A(cf)
Minor Premise	Some animals are not felines.	O(af)
Conclusion	Some animals are cats	I(ac)

First, The Major Premise, A(cf) has two diagram-sets.

Figure 4.1

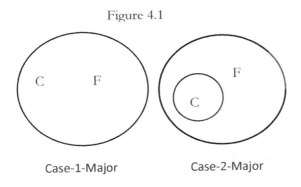

Case-1-Major   Case-2-Major

Next, The Minor Premise displayed in Figure 4.2, O(af) is represented by 3 sets of diagrams as Chart 3.1 indicates. In other words, "Some a is not f " shows up in Cases 3, 4, and 5 (Line O) of Chart 3.1. Begin with the Case-3-Minor diagram and impose it on each of the diagrams above. This procedure results in 4 outcomes: ONE, when the Case-3-Minor is imposed on the first Case-1-Major diagram above, THREE, when the Case-3-Minor is imposed on the second Case-2-Major diagram above. (With the last imposition there are 3 possible configurations.) Ask of each: "Is I(ac) true every time?"

Case-3-Minor

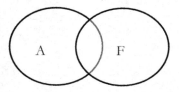

Figure 4.2

Imposition of the Case-3-Minor on Case-1-Major yields Figure 4.3.

Figure 4.3

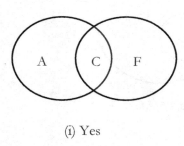

(i) Yes

Is I(ac)? Some a is c? Answer: YES

Imposing the Case-3-Minor on Case-2-Major produces the three configurations of Figures 4.4a, 4.4b, and 4.4c that follow in that order.

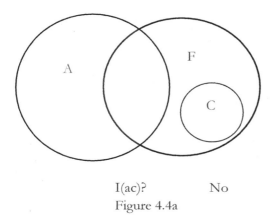

I(ac)?   No

Figure 4.4a

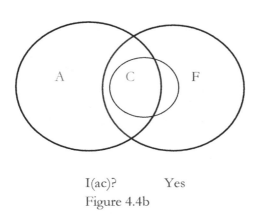

I(ac)?   Yes

Figure 4.4b

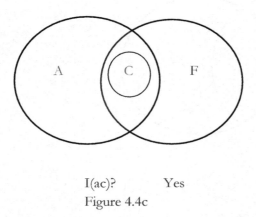

I(ac)?   Yes
Figure 4.4c

Is I(ac)? No in Figure 4.4a. Yes in Figures 4.4 b & c.

There are two more diagrams, Case-4-Minor and Case-5-Minor, to impose or map on the two A(cf) diagrams (Cases 1 and 2) of the major premise. However, you need not draw all of the diagrams if one imposition of diagrams reveals invalidity, as in Figure 4.4a above. If the answer to the question is "NO" for any instance, then the syllogism is invalid.

Another example follows using Frame: AEE-1

    Major Premise   All who wear tuxedos are civilized.   A(tc)

    Minor Premise   No zombies wear tuxedos.   E(zt)

    Conclusion   No zombies are civilized   E(zc)

First, The Major Premise, A(tc) has two diagrams, Cases 1 and 2. (See Chart 3.1)

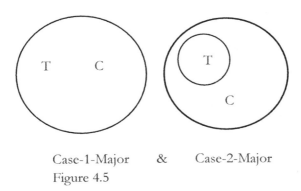

Case-1-Major   &   Case-2-Major
Figure 4.5

Next, The Minor Premise, E(zt) has one set of two circles, Case 5 in Chart 3.1:

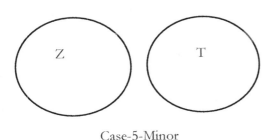

Case-5-Minor
Figure 4.6

Imposition of the Case-5-Minor on each of the major diagrams above, Case-1-Major and Case-2-Major, yields the following outcomes displayed in Figures 4.7 and 4.8.(i and ii on the first diagram, Case-1-Major, and iii and iv on second diagram, Case-2-Major).

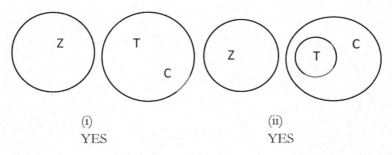

Figure 4.7

Is E(zc)? YES, in both (i) and (ii).

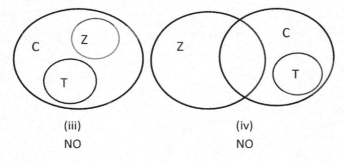

Figure 4.8

Is E(zc)? The answer is NO in both (iii) and (iv) of Figure 4.8 above. In (iii), all of z falls inside of c; therefore, it is false that no z is c. In (iv), some z overlaps c; therefore, it is false that no z is c.

To repeat: The conclusion E(zc) is not true every time; it is true in (i) and (ii), but not in (iii) and (iv). Therefore, the syllogism is invalid.

There are more complicated frames in which the likelihood of mistakes, or omitting a single possibility is higher. Therefore, knowledge of the rules and their application to determine validity is clearly an advantage to be preferred.

This last example tests the valid frame Celarent, EAE-1: E(ba) A(cb) < E(ca) using diagrams.

First, The Major Premise, E(ba) has one set of two circles as drawn in Figure 4.9:

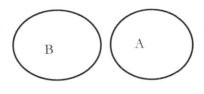

Case 5 Major

Figure 4.9

Next, The Minor Premise, A(cb) has two sets diagrams as seen in Figure 4.10:

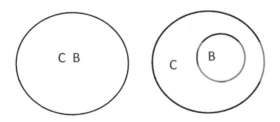

Case-1-Minor   &   Case-2-Minor

Figure 4.10

Results: Two sets in Figure 4.11, (i) and (ii) below. Number (i) is the result of imposing the first diagram, Case-1-Minor to Case-5-Major. Number (ii) is the result of imposing the second diagram, Case-2-Minor to the Case-5-Major.

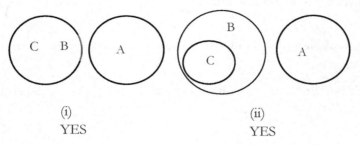

(i)
YES

(ii)
YES

Figure 4.11

E(ca)? The answer is YES in both (i) and (ii) above. In (i), it is true that *no c is a.* In (ii), it is true that *no c is a.* Clearly, E(ca) is true every time; therefore, the syllogism is valid. Remember, an implication or argument is valid if and only if the conclusion is true every time the premises are true – every time!

Nonstandard Syllogisms

A syllogism may fail to be in standard form in a number of ways. The first pair of examples below are syllogisms containing more than three, but not unrelated, terms. Moreover, their propositions are not in the proper order: major premise, minor premise, and then conclusion. The second set of examples discusses syllogisms with a suppressed premise or conclusion (enthymemes). Finally, a third type of nonstandard syllogism, sorites, is discussed.

Syllogisms Containing More Than 3 Terms

The arguments below have more than three terms each. They are not in proper order: major premise first, minor premise second, then conclusion last. The task is to reduce the number of terms to three, if possible, making certain that each term is used in the same sense. This can be done by obverting the second premise of the first argument and the first premise and the conclusion of the second argument.

Argument 1

1ˢᵗ Premise   All inexpensive things are poorly constructed.

2ⁿᵈ Premise   All German cars are expensive.

Conclusion   ∴ No poorly constructed things are German cars.

Reducing the terms to three, and if necessary re-ordering the premises can be done in one operation. Instead to simplify the process, two steps are described for each argument. (Let *a* for Major Term; *b* for Middle Term; *c* for the Minor Term.)

Step 1: Obvert 2nd Premise to "No German cars are inexpensive." (Obverted, the A form becomes E form)

Step 2: Correct order of premises (major then minor).

Major	No German cars are inexpensive.	E(ab)
Minor	All inexpensive things are poorly constructed.	A(bc)
Conclusion	∴ No poorly constructed things are German cars.	E(ca)

EAE-4, Invalid by Rule #2 (The minor term, poorly-constructed-things, is undistributed in the premise but distributed in the conclusion.)

Argument 2

1st Premise	Some of the stolen books are not replaceable.
2nd Premise	No irreplaceable things are deductible.
Conclusion	∴ Some of the stolen books are non-deductible.

To reduce the number of terms in this second argument, obvert the first premise and the conclusion, then correct the order of the premises.

Premise 1: Some of the stolen books are irreplaceable. (obverted, O form to I form)

Conclusion: Some of the stolen books are not deductible. (obverted, I form to O form)

Major	No irreplaceable things are deductible.	E(ba)
Minor	Some of the stolen books are irreplaceable.	I(cb)

Conclusion   Some of the stolen books are not deductible.   O(ca)

EIO-1, Valid. The tests of Rules 1 through 5 are met in this example.

Enthymemes

An otherwise perfectly valid categorical syllogism may appear not to be so when one of its propositions is suppressed or understood but not explicitly stated. Such an argument is known as an *enthymeme*.

Three examples follow where a = major term; b = middle term, and c = minor term. The first enthymeme has a suppressed major premise, the second, a suppressed minor premise, and the third, a suppressed conclusion.

Suppressed Major Premise Example

Enthymeme 1: Some NFL quarterbacks are good passers because some NFL quarterbacks have strong throwing arms.

Minor Premise	Some NFL quarterbacks have strong throwing arms.	I(cb)
Conclusion	∴ Some NFL quarterbacks are good passers.	I(ca)
Missing Major	All persons with strong throwing arms are good passers.	A(ba)
Syllogism	A(ba) I(cb) < I(ca).	

Valid, AII-1 Darii

Suppressed Minor Premise Example

Enthymeme 2: No one in his right mind claims infallibility, for only perfect persons can claim infallibility.

Major Premise	All persons claiming infallibility are perfect persons.	A(ab)
Conclusion	∴ No person in his right mind claims infallibility.	E(ca)
Missing Minor	No person in his right mind claims to be a perfect person.	E(cb)
Syllogism	A(ab) E(cb) < E(ca)	

Valid, AEE-2, Camestres

Suppressed Conclusion Example

Enthymeme 3: No fair-minded person is capricious and some capricious people are irresponsible.

Major Premise	No fair-minded person is capricious	E(ab)
Minor Premise	Some capricious people are irresponsible.	I(bc)
Missing Conclusion	∴ Some irresponsible people are not fair-minded	O(ca)
Syllogism	E(ab) I(bc) < O(ca).	

Valid: EIO-4, Fresison

Sorites

Nonstandard syllogisms may contain more than the required three forms. A *sorites* consists of a series of propositions in which the predicate of each is the subject of the next. The conclusion consists of the first subject and the last predicate. The chain of propositions is arranged in pairs of premises to make explicit the suppressed conclusion, thereby revealing the syllogism. The validity of the entire chain will depend on the validity of each syllogism in the chain.

In this example, a = atheists; n = nihilists; m = misologists; u = unreasonable (people); and f = fools. What can be concluded, given the following four propositions?

i	All atheists are nihilists.	A(an)
ii	All nihilists are misologists	A(nm)
iii	All misologists are unreasonable	A(mu)
iv	All unreasonable ones are fools.	A(uf)

One interpretation takes "nihilists" in the first two propositions as the middle term, and rearranging the premises, yields the first syllogism.

Major	(ii)	All nihilists are misologists.	A(nm)

Minor	(i)	All atheists are nihilists.	A(an)
1st Conclusion		∴All atheists are misologists.	A(am) (made explicit)

Using the 1st Conclusion as a premise in conjunction with the third proposition, and rearranging the premises, yields the second syllogism.

Major	(iii)	All misologists are unreasonable.	A(mu)
1st Conclusion (Minor)		All atheists are misologists.	A(am)
2nd Conclusion		∴ All atheists are unreasonable.	A(au) (made explicit)

Using the 2nd Conclusion as a premise in conjunction with the fourth proposition, and rearranging the premises, yields the third syllogism.

Major	(iv)	All unreasonable ones are fools.	A(uf)
2nd Conclusion (Minor)		All atheists are unreasonable.	A(au)
3rd Conclusion		∴ All atheists are fools.	A(af)**

(**Note: The "3rd Conclusion above is Made Explicit)

A sorites is valid if and only if each syllogism forming a part of the sorites is valid. Each syllogism above is an instance of AAA-1, Barbara. Therefore, the sorites as a whole is valid.

In evaluating a sorites, keep in mind these requirements.

1. If a conclusion is negative, then one and only one of the premises must be negative.
2. If a conclusion is affirmative, all of the propositions must be affirmative.
3. If a conclusion is universal, all of the premises must be universal.
4. A particular conclusion calls for not more than one particular premise.

Summary

This chapter described in some detail syllogistic reasoning. The value of the study of syllogisms cannot be overemphasized because of all the arguments in science, religion, politics, and history "the greater proportion by far is syllogistic in form." (Clark, G. H. Logic, HC ed., p. 53)

In this chapter, we analyzed and illustrated some of the more important aspects of syllogistic reasoning. We described the basic elements of syllogisms: the minor, middle, and major terms of the syllogism; the basic structure of a syllogism consisting of a major premise, a minor premise and a conclusion; the meaning of the conventional form of a syllogism; the 24 moods and figures of valid syllogisms; and the significance of the corresponding frame names.

Three methods for proving the validity of syllogisms were explained: Five Rules to determine validity of an implication or argument; the Deduction Method to deduce valid implications (theorems); and Venn Diagrams to display validity using circles.

The first method made use of five (necessary and sufficient) rules that each syllogism must meet if it is to qualify as valid.

The second method deduced 7 of the 24 valid syllogisms as theorems. They were deduced from 2 axioms using two principles that functioned as decision rules. The first principle holds that a valid implication results when a valid implication's premise and conclusion are interchanged and contradicted. The second principle states that in any valid implication, "weakening" its conclusion, or "strengthening" its premise results in a valid implication. These principles, when applied to the two axioms, enabled the valid deductions of theorems.

As a feature of the deduction method, we illustrated the *reductio ad absurdum* (RAA) procedure wherein one assumes the falsity of the conclusion of an implication as an added premise in order to deduce a contradiction. The deduction of a contradiction in this manner proves that the assumption of a false conclusion was unwarranted. Therefore, the original implication's conclusion (not its contradictory) must be true. The original implication is valid.

The third method, Venn Diagrams (Euler Circles), used the definition of valid inference to obtain a visual display of a valid or invalid syllogistic inference. An inference is valid whenever the form of the conclusion is true every time the forms of the premises are. If the mapping of the minor premise's diagram(s) onto the major premise diagram(s) results in the truth of the conclusion for each required mapping, then the syllogism is valid. If any single mapping of minor to major diagrams fails the test, the syllogism is invalid.

Additional confirmation of invalidity (or validity) is obtained by application of the five rules, and/or the identification of the syllogism's mood and figure with one of the frame names for valid syllogisms.

Finally, three nonstandard syllogisms were illustrated: a syllogism with more than three terms; an enthymeme; and a sorites. With the first, a reduction of the terms to three univocal terms required of standard syllogisms was achieved by the use of obversion and/or contraposition on premises and/or conclusion. With enthymemes, the suppressed or implied missing premise or conclusion was made explicit, the argument's propositions reordered if necessary (major, minor, conclusion), then the syllogism was tested for validity by application of the five rules. With sorites the task was more complicated, but nevertheless useful, since it provides a platform for the formulation and testing of syllogistic reasoning. A sorites is a chain of related propositions in which the predicate of each is the subject of the next, until the chain ends with a proposition that consists of the first subject and the last predicate. The chain is arranged in pairs of statements to make explicit the suppressed conclusion, revealing the syllogism. The chain of syllogisms is valid if, and only if, each syllogism in the chain is a valid syllogism. Guidelines for evaluating sorites were described in four requirements for validity.

Review

All of the syllogisms below are invalid. Each invalid argument illustrates the violation of one of the five rules for determining the validity of a syllogism. Which rule does each transgress? Does each example violate one and only one rule? Does understanding the particular rule violated suggest what may be done to attain a valid syllogism?

1. Because All hedonists are irrational, and All irrationalists are misologists, does it follow that Some misologists are not hedonists?

2. If All men are intelligent, and All men are bipeds, therefore, is it the case that All bipeds are intelligent?

3. Granted that Some fruit is not sweet, and that All pears are sweet. Can we conclude that Some pears are fruit?

4. Assume that No dictators are benevolent, and Some kings are not dictators. Does it follow that Some kings are not benevolent?

5. All men have two legs, and All apes have two legs. Conclusion: All apes are men?

Exercise 4.1: Definition of Terms Standard Syllogism

Instructions: Fill in the blank in each statement with the letter of the most correct answer.

a	conversion per accidens	h	reductio ad absurdum
b	first figure	i	second figure
c	major premise	j	simple conversion
d	major term	k	syllogism
e	middle term	l	third figure
f	minor premise	m	validity
g	minor term	n	None of These

STATEMENTS	
1	A _____ is an inference with two premises and three terms, each appearing twice but never twice in the same proposition.
2	The _____ is the predicate of the conclusion of a standard syllogism.
3	The _____ is the subject of the conclusion of a standard syllogism.

4	The term that occurs in both premises, but not in the conclusion is the _____ .
5	The _____ is the one that contains the major term.
6	The _____ is the one that contains the minor term.
7	The lower case letter "s" in the name of a valid frame means _____ of the preceding form.
8	The lower case "p" in the name of a valid frame means _____.
9	The _____ is the subject term of the major premise and the predicate term of the minor premise of a standard syllogism.
10	The _____ is the predicate of both premises of a standard syllogism.
11	The _____ is the subject of both premises of a standard syllogism.
12	The lower case "k" in the name of a valid frame means _____.

Exercise 4.2: Syllogisms

Instructions: Determine the validity of each argument. Mark V for valid; I for invalid. If an argument is valid, cite the frame name. If an argument is invalid, cite which of the five rules is violated.

ARGUMENTS		V/I
1	All thinking beings are existing beings. I am a thinking being; therefore, I am an existing being.	
2	Some good Christians are communists because Some good Christians practice what they preach; and All communists practice what they preach."	
3	Suppose someone argues: No logic students swallow propaganda. The premises are: (1) No logic students are stupid; and (2) All stupid people swallow propaganda.	
4	All whom the Son makes free are free indeed, because all who know the truth are free indeed; and all whom the Son makes free know the truth.	
5	Descriptive sciences have no place for evaluations. Psychology is a descriptive science, among others.	

	Therefore, psychology has no place for evaluations.	
6	All that God does is good. God clearly predestinates evil. Therefore, God does good in predestinating evil.	
7	No person who knows the Truth is a slave of sin. All whom the Son makes free are persons who know the Truth. Therefore, no person whom the Son makes free is a slave of sin.	
8	Does it make sense to argue that some poor scholars are theologians because all theologians are former seminary students, and some seminary students were poor scholars?	
9	Our sense organs change, either by reason of aging or by reason of disease, leading to deception. These changes usually occur without our knowing it. Therefore, we are often or almost always deceived.	
10	Every system of philosophy must have a starting point, an axiom or set of axioms, for otherwise it could not start. Starting points cannot be demonstrated. Therefore, every system of thought must be based on an indemonstrable axiom.	

Exercise 4.3 Deduction Definitions

Instructions: Fill in the blank(s) in each statement with the letter of the most correct answer.

a	axioms	e	strengthened form
b	theorem	f	weakened form
c	Principle 1 Deduction	g	Five Rules (Validity)
d	Principle 2 Deduction	h	necessary & sufficient

STATEMENTS	
1	_____ are never deduced because they are the starting points of all deduction.
2	_____ states that if in any valid implication the premise and the conclusion be interchanged and contradicted, the result is a valid implication.
3	_____ states that if any valid implication its premise be strengthened or its conclusion weakened, a valid implication will result.
4	The premise of a valid implication is a _____ of its consequent and the conclusion is a _____ of its premise.
5	There are _____ by which any standard syllogism may be tested for validity.
6	One proves a _____ by applying rules to the axioms.
7	The five rules are _____ , if you cannot do without them and there is at least one invalid syllogism to which the given rule alone applies.

5 ADDITIONAL ARGUMENT FORMS

The definition of argument, as a connected series of reasons intended to establish a conclusion or position, embraces argument forms other than the syllogism studied in the last chapter. A primer on syllogistic reasoning should introduce the beginning student to other forms of argument that are based on the foundations of immediate and syllogistic inferences. To this end, discussion in this chapter will cover five additional argument forms and two associated formal fallacies. Two of the five argument forms are best known by their Latin names. Here is the first.

Modus Ponens

Modus Ponens is also known as hypothetical syllogism, or the constructive hypothetical syllogism, to distinguish it from another form of hypothetical syllogism described later in the chapter.

Syllogisms , and generally arguments, can be expressed as conditionals, i. e., as "If ..., then ..." statements. The conjunction of the premises of an argument becomes the antecedent of the conditional statement, and the conclusion of the argument becomes the consequent. (Another notation, makes use of " $\supset$ " instead of " $<$ " to symbolize the "if ..., then ..." relation.) Thus, Modus Ponens expressed as a conditional or an implication becomes: "if a then b, *and* a; therefore b."

Using the symbols of logical notation yields the following.

$\{ [(a < b)$ & $a] < b \}$, or $\{ [(a \supset b)$ & $a] \supset b \}$

Braces, brackets, and parentheses are punctuation symbols to make clear the relations in the expression.

A dot or ampersand denotes the relation of conjunction or, if absent between variables, assumed. Thus (ab) is a conjunction (a and b). Disjunction uses " v " or " + " to connect disjuncts in an expression in this fashion: (a v b) or (a + b).

Modus Ponens, as with all of the other argument forms in this chapter except the dilemma, consists of two premises and a conclusion. A single letter of the alphabet used consistently, stands for a particular proposition in an argument. Any upper or lower case letter of the alphabet will do, but that same letter must be used consistently for other instances of the same proposition within the argument. Remember, a proposition is the meaning of a declarative sentence.

The form of Modus Ponens is:

a implies b, (or if a then b)

a is true

∴ b is true

Given an implication (or conditional) as a premise with the antecedent of the implication as a second premise, one can then validly infer the consequent of the implication as a conclusion. The order of the premises is of no consequence, although the implication comes first in the order of premises.

Here is another example.

If John stole the money, then he has a guilty conscience. He stole the money. Therefore, he has a guilty conscience.

In symbolic form, where " a " stands for "John stole the money" and "b" stands for "he has a guilty conscience."

a < b

a

∴b

Modus Tollens

Modus Tollens or destructive hypothetical syllogism has this form:

a implies b, (or if a then b)

b is false

∴a is false

In words: starting with a conditional as a premise and the denial of its consequent as another premise, it is valid to infer the denial of the antecedent of the conditional as conclusion.

To illustrate: If this beaker contains acid, then it will turn litmus paper red. It does not turn litmus paper red. Therefore, this beaker does not contain acid.

In symbolic form:

a < b

not-b

∴not-a

(Negation is symbolized in some texts by " ~ " or the prime symbol after the propositional variable, thus: " a is false " or "not-a " becomes " ~ a" or " a ' ", read as "not a" or " a is false ".)

Formal Fallacies

A fallacy is a mistake in reasoning. A formal fallacy is a mistake in the form of the argument itself; it is an invalid argument form. There are two formal fallacies sometimes mistaken for Modus Ponens and Modus Tollens. These are (1) the Fallacy of Affirming or Asserting the Consequent; and (2) the Fallacy of Denying the Antecedent.

Fallacy of Denying the Antecedent

An implication (conditional) as premise and the denial of its antecedent as another premise do not imply a conclusion. To claim that such premises imply a conclusion is a fallacy. Thus, to argue that since *a implies b*, where *a is false*, therefore, *b is false* is to commit the Fallacy of Denying the Antecedent.

To illustrate: If Jane is a good speller, then she can spell "syllogism." Jane is not a good speller. Therefore, Jane cannot spell "syllogism." Note that even though Jane is a poor speller, she may happen nevertheless to know how to spell *syllogism*.

Fallacy of Affirming the Consequent

An implication (conditional) as premise and affirming the consequent as another premise do not imply the antecedent of the implication as a conclusion. Thus, to argue that *if a implies b and b is true; therefore, a is true* is to commit the Fallacy of Affirming the Consequent.

To illustrate: If he is honest, he will not lie. He will not lie. Therefore, he is honest. Note: A mere instance of not lying does not logically establish the virtue of honesty.

The next Chapter has a section that shows the invalidity of the Fallacy of Asserting or Affirming the Consequent by Truth-Table analysis. A similar Truth-Table analysis will show the invalidity of the Fallacy of Denying the Antecedent.

Transitive Hypothetical Syllogism

In Chapter 3, Immediate Inference, the description of transitive relationships anticipated this argument form. Some logic books cite this form of argument as *hypothetical syllogism*. To avoid the confusion of assigning the same name to different argument forms, this argument form's name includes the word "transitive" in its name. As with all of these argument forms, the order of the premises is of no consequence.

Its form is:

> a implies b, (if a then b)
>
> b implies c, (if b then c)
>
> ∴ a implies c, (if a then c)

To illustrate: "If students cheat on exams, this means that the exams are too difficult. If the exams are too difficult, the instructor should be disqualified. Therefore, if students cheat on exams, the instructor should be disqualified."

Note: Our illustration contains one or more false propositions. While the argument is unsound, it is nevertheless valid.

Disjunctive Hypothetical Syllogism

A disjunction is an *either ...*, *or ...* statement. As we know, **or** has more than one sense; in fact, it has three.

(1) "Heaven or Hell" as the title of a sermon, means one to the exclusion of the other but not both. This is the exclusive sense of **or**.

(2) In "she studied logic or she is a home-schooler," we illustrate the inclusive sense of **or**. The student may have both studied logic and been home-educated. The inclusive sense of **or** means at least one, not requiring, but permitting both.

(3) In "the Gospel, or Good News" one has the synonymous sense of **or** in mind.

The **or** of Disjunctive Hypothetical Syllogism is the inclusive sense. The argument form is:

> either a or b
>
> a is false
>
> ∴ b is true

In a sentence: An inclusive sense disjunction and a denial of one of its disjuncts imply the other disjunct as a conclusion.

To illustrate: Either he enjoys telling falsehoods or he is afraid to tell the truth. He does not enjoy telling falsehoods. Therefore, he is afraid to tell the truth.

The above form is the "standard form." The definition of Disjunctive Hypothetical Syllogism does not rule out any number of nonstandard versions. Thus, the following nonstandard version qualifies as Disjunctive Hypothetical Syllogism.

$a \lor b'$

b

∴ a

(The exclusive sense of *or* means "either a or b, but not both a and b.")

The Dilemma

The argument form known as the dilemma is perhaps the most complex of the five argument forms. Gordon Clark defines a dilemma as *an argument whose conclusion follows or appears to follow from contradictory premises.*

There are two varieties of this form.

The constructive form (CD).

Premise 1: (if a then b)

Premise 2: (if c then d)

Premise 3: (a or c)

Conclusion: ∴ (b or d)

The destructive form (DD).

Premise 1: (if a then b)

Premise 2: (if c then d)

Premise 3: (b' or d')

Conclusion: ∴ (a' or c')

Some reminders about logical notation follow.

Using " < " for implies and " ∨ " for the inclusive sense of *or*, the form can be expressed as an implication.

(Note: The absence of a logical connective between propositional variables assumes a conjunction. Also note, the prime " ' " when attached to a letter is a denial of the proposition represented by that letter, or of the entire expression, if a compound.)

The bold " **<** " is the major logical connective, here used to distinguish the antecedent premises set from the consequent conclusion of the implication.

(Use of parentheses and brackets serve to make explicit the relations of the elements of the expression.)

The constructive form of the dilemma (CD) is:

$$[(a < b) (c < d) (a \vee c)] < (b \vee d).$$

The destructive form of the dilemma (DD) is:

$$[(a < b) (c < d) (b' \vee d')] < (a' \vee c').$$

The next two arguments are examples of defective dilemmas that serve to identify important precautions when evaluating dilemmas.

First, an argument posing as a Constructive Dilemma example:

If you do nothing, you will be considered an accomplice by your silence.

If you resist, then you will be labeled a trouble-maker.

Now, either you do nothing, or you resist.

Thus, either you will be considered an accomplice or a trouble-maker.

Second, an argument posing as a Destructive Dilemma example:

If I lie, I will be considered an accomplice.

If I protest, I am labeled a trouble-maker.

Either I am not an accomplice or I am not a trouble-maker.

Thus, either I am not a liar or I am not a protestor.

First Precaution: The form of a dilemma assumes that the first two statements are valid logical inferences. If one or the other of the "if ... then" premises is an invalid inference, the dilemma fails as a valid argument form. Thus, any dilemma whose first two premises do not passing our tests for valid inference fails to quality as a genuine valid dilemma.

Second Precaution: The form of a dilemma assumes that the disjunction, the third premise, is a complete disjunction. If the disjunction is incomplete, i.e., allows for a third possibility, the argument fails as a valid dilemma.

To repeat for emphasis: An argument may have the form of a dilemma but on examination fail to qualify as genuine. The conditional premises must meet the tests for valid inference and the disjunction must not allow for a third possibility. If either of these are evident, the argument fails as a genuine dilemma.

Keep in mind also that the various letters of the dilemma are propositional variables. The identical proposition must be substituted, for example, for the letter *a* wherever it appears in the dilemma, and similarly for each of the other variables. Otherwise, the dilemma does not so much fail, as never gets started.

Suppose we examine the second argument that was put forward as an example of a Destructive Dilemma to illustrate the precautions named above.

If I lie, I will be considered an accomplice.

If I protest, I am labeled a trouble-maker.

The first precaution states that the implications must be valid inferences. Does either premise express a necessary inference?

An examination of the premises reveals that no necessary inference is involved in either one. Rather, what is asserted in each is a definition of a condition in the form of an implication. Thus "to lie" means "to be considered an accomplice." And "to protest" means "to be labeled a trouble-maker." As such, these implications stipulate meanings, not logical relations between antecedents and consequents.

In short, that "X lies" does not necessarily imply that "X is an accomplice." And that "X is a trouble-maker " is not a necessary consequence of "X protests." Moreover, neither conditional is a necessary consequence of the other. These conditional statements do not rise to the level for any test of validity simply because a logical relation between their antecedents and consequents is absent.

Summarizing. The implications are not valid inferences. Indeed, there is no logical connection between the antecedent and the consequent of the implication to which a test for validity can be applied. This example fails to meet the requirements of a genuine dilemma.

The second precaution states that the disjunction (the 3rd premise) must be a complete disjunction.

Either I am not an accomplice or I am not a trouble-maker.

The disjunction's disjuncts are not obviously mutually exclusive options. These options do not exhaust all other alternatives. For example, one could be both, i.e., not an accomplice and not a trouble-maker. Thus, the disjunction is not a complete, since it reasonably allows for other options or alternatives. Once again, this example fails to meet the requirements of a genuine dilemma.

To complete our examination of the argument, it should be noted that the terms of the argument may not be, and must be, univocal, not only in any dilemma, but in any argument.

Thus, either I am not a liar or I am not a protestor.

The terms in the conclusion are not identical to the terms in the premises. However, even if the terms of the conclusion were identical with those in the premises, the denials in the conclusion are ambiguous. The terms "not-a-liar" and "not-a-protestor" may or may not mean the same as the associated terms in the premises.

This argument as an example of a Destructive Dilemma fails to qualify as a genuine dilemma. Moreover, the conclusion is not a necessary consequence of the premises on any other grounds. Therefore, the argument is not valid. (A similar analysis of the first argument, offered as an example of a Constructive Dilemma, will show that it does not qualify as a genuine dilemma either.)

We shall close this chapter with discussions of three relationships, each showing the interdefinability of:

(1) conjunction and disjunction;

(2) implication and conjunction; and

(3) implication and disjunction.

"Interdefinability," in this context, means that a conjunction can be expressed as a disjunction; an implication can be expressed as a conjunction; and an implication can be expressed as a disjunction.

Conjunction and Disjunction

The denial of a conjunction is equivalent to (equal to) a disjunction of the denials of the propositions. In addition, the denial of a disjunction is equivalent to a conjunction of the denials of the propositions. The relation is symmetrical; so, the order is of no consequence.

As before, " $\vee$ " is inclusive disjunction; "(ab)" or "(ab) (cd)" are conjunctions; " ′ " stands for the denial of the letter to which it is attached; and " $=$ " stands for "is equivalent to " or " is equal to."

The Denial of a Conjunction

$$(ab)' = (a' \vee b')$$

The two propositions that follow are logically equivalent:

Proposition 1: It is not the case that you ignore logic, and you will enjoy peace of mind.

Proposition 2: Either you do not ignore logic, or you will not enjoy peace of mind.

The denial the conjunction, (a and b), is equivalent to the disjunction of the two separately denied, (not-a or not-b). In turn, the disjunction, $(a' \vee b')$ is equivalent to a denial of the conjunction yielding $(ab)'$.

Suppose $(a' b')$ is denied as in $(a' b')'$.

This last expression is equivalent to (a v b).

(Note: See Chapter 6 on Truth Tables for demonstrations of logically equivalent expressions.)

The Denial of a Disjunction

$$(a \vee b)' = (a' b')$$

The denial of a disjunction is logically equivalent to a conjunction of the variables denied.

To summarize: The denial of a conjunction is equal to a disjunction of the denied variables. The denial of a disjunction is equal or equivalent to the conjunction of the two propositions separately denied. (The next chapter will show logical equivalence of the above and the following expressions using truth tables.)

Implication and Conjunction

An implication (conditional) is logically equivalent to a denial of a conjunction when the conjunction consists of the antecedent proposition and the denial of the consequent proposition of the implication. The form is as follows:

$$(a < b) = (ab')'$$

The implication, "if a then b" is equal or logically equivalent to "it is not the case that a and not-b."

The following propositions are logically equivalent:

Proposition 1: If you are a good student, then you will master logic.

Proposition 2: It is not the case that you are a good student and you will not master logic.

Implication and Disjunction

An implication is equivalent to a disjunction consisting of the denial of the antecedent as one disjunct and the consequent of the implication as the other disjunct. It has this form:

$$(a < b) = (a' \lor b)$$

The implication, "if a then b" is equal or equivalent to "either not-a or b." The following propositions are logically equivalent:

Proposition 1: If you are a good student, then you will master logic.

Proposition 2: Either you are not a good student, or you will master logic.

These relations between conjunction and disjunction, implication and conjunction, and implication and disjunction have names that at this stage would constitute extra baggage for the student. The important lesson here is to realize that conjunction, disjunction, and implication are interdefinable. The relations between conjunction, disjunction, and implication when formulated according to our procedures, demonstrate the power of symbols for the expression of complex meanings.

For example, how many lines of English do you think are necessary to express the relations in these three expressions?

$$(a < b) = (a' \lor b) = (a\ b')'$$

Truth-Table analysis in Chapter Six, will show that these three expressions are logically equivalent (interdefinable).

We are now in a position to express in more definitive language the relations between the laws of logic alluded to in Chapter One. There, it was noted that the law of contradiction encompasses the other two. We could have said "contained the other two." The ambiguity of the verbs "to encompass" or "to contain" is eliminated by this:

$$(a\ a')' = (a' \lor a) = (a < a)$$

It reads: "not both a and not-a" is equivalent to "either not-a or a" is equivalent to "a implies a."

Given the logical equivalence of the three -- to deny one is to deny all; to uphold one is to uphold all. (Truth Table methods in the next chapter demonstrate the validity of the interdefinability of these expressions.)

Summary

The aim of this chapter has been to introduce and provide some examples of additional argument forms: Modus Ponens, Modus Tollens, Transitive Hypothetical Syllogism, Disjunctive Hypothetical Syllogism, and two versions of the Dilemma, the Constructive Dilemma and the Destructive Dilemma. The argument forms described were the standard forms for each class of argument. There are nonstandard versions of each type of argument form. We did not illustrate the nonstandard variety for each case; however, we did offer a nonstandard example of Hypothetical Disjunctive Syllogism. There are nonstandard versions for each argument form. Our definitions of these argument forms in this chapter allow for nonstandard versions.

This chapter closes with important truths about the relation between conjunction and disjunction, and each of these with implication. The definitions for the relationships establish the *interdefinability* of conjunction and disjunction, implication and conjunction, and implication and disjunction. "Interdefinable" means "logically equivalent." These relations form the basis for showing that the law of contradiction "contains" the other two laws: $(a\ a')' = (a' \vee a) = (a < a)$. The expressions are logically equivalent, but the law of contradiction is supreme. Without the law of contradiction, the law of excluded middle and the law of identity lose their significance. These three laws are foundational for the truth table analyses of arguments in the next chapter.

Review

1. What are the basic differences and similarities between the argument forms modus ponens and modus tollens?

2. Construct an ordinary language argument illustrating the fallacy of affirming the consequent in which the premises are obviously true and the conclusion obviously false.

3. Construct an example of the fallacy of denying the antecedent in which the premises are obviously true and the conclusion obviously false.

4. What are the disjunctive and conjunctive forms of this implication: $(a' \vee b) < c'$?

5. This example from Gordon Clark's book, *Logic*:

If I vote the Democratic ticket, I shall encourage war and inflation. If I vote Republican, I encourage depression and unemployment. But I must vote either Democratic or Republican. So I am forced to encourage war or unemployment. (HC ed., p. 99.)

Evaluate this argument form according to possible mistakes about dilemmas.

Exercise 5.1 Additional Argument Forms

Instructions: Fill in the blanks in each statement with the letter of the correct answer.

a	disjunctive syllogism	f	transitive syllogism
b	affirming the consequent	g	modus ponens
c	complete	h	modus tollens
d	denying the antecedent	i	interdefinable
e	dilemma	j	valid

STATEMENTS	
1	_____ has an implication as a premise and the antecedent of the implication as a second premise from which one concludes the consequent of the first.
2	The form of argument in which: X implies Y, and the 2nd premise is: Y is false; and the conclusion is therefore: X is false, is known as _____.
3	"X implies Y, and Y is true; therefore, X is true." This argument form exemplifies the fallacy of _____.
4	Argument Form: X implies Y, and X is false; therefore, Y is false, is the fallacy of _____.
5	The _____ form consists of premises: X ∨ Y, and X is false, to conclude: Y is true.

6	The argument form $[(X < Y) (Z < W) (X \lor Z)] < (Y \lor W)$ is known as a(n) _____.
7	If the first two premises of a dilemma are not _____ inferences, the dilemma fails.
8	The disjunction premise of a dilemma must be a _____ disjunction or the dilemma fails.
9	The formula: $(XY)' = (X' \lor Y')$ shows that conjunction and disjunction are _____.
10	The implication $[(X < Y) (Y < Z)] < (X < Z)$ is known as _____.

Exercise 5.2 Arguments & Definitions

Instructions: Determine the validity of each of the following.

1	If the party now in power wins the next election, then in all probability we shall go to war somewhere in the world. In all probability we shall go to war somewhere in the world. Therefore, the party now in power wins the next election.
2	If Jane is a good speller, then she can spell "syllogism." Jane is not a good speller. Therefore, Jane cannot spell "syllogism."
3	If students cheat on exams, this means the exams are too difficult. If the exams are too difficult, the instructor should be disqualified. Therefore, if students cheat on exams, the instructor should be disqualified.
4	If John stole the money, then he has a guilty conscience. He stole the money. Therefore, he has a guilty conscience.
5	If she is honest, she will not lie. She did not lie. Consequently, she is not dishonest.
6.	Either this course is easily mastered, or it should not be listed in General Education. Either this course should be listed in General Education, or it should be abolished from the entire curriculum. Therefore, if this course is not easily mastered, it should be abolished from the entire curriculum.
7	If you do nothing, then you will be considered an accomplice. If you resist, then you will be accused of provoking disagreement. Either you do nothing, or you resist. Thus, either you will be

	considered an accomplice, or you will be accused of provoking disagreement.
8	Either this beaker does not contain acid, or it will turn litmus paper red. It does not turn blue litmus paper red. Therefore, the beaker does not contain acid.
9	If A then B is equivalent to Not-A or B is equivalent to it is Not the case that both A and not-B.
10	The denial of $A \vee B$ is equivalent to both *Not-A and Not-B*; and the *denial of both A and B* is equivalent to *either Not-A or Not-B*.

6 TRUTH TABLES

Truth tables are heuristic methods for the analysis of propositional forms and arguments. They function as schemata for the analysis of forms and relations among them. The basis of truth tables is the fact that every proposition is either true or false.

Previous chapters defined the logical connectives used in creating truth functions. In this chapter, we define the logical connectives using truth tables. We then provide instructions for constructing the appropriate truth table followed by a number of applications.

Logical Connectives

Some logical connectives were introduced in Chapter Two. The connectives join simple statements to form compound statements. In Chapter Two, and since then, "and," "or," "implies," and "not" have been used to connect simple statements into compounds of propositional forms. We shall now express their meanings by means of truth tables. The laws of logic (the Law of Identity, the Law of Excluded Middle, and the Law of Contradiction or Non-Contradiction) are the basis for all truth tables.

The law that states that every proposition is either true or false is expressed in truth table fashion as follows.

Negation

Rows	p	p′	(p′)′
1	T	F	T
2	F	T	F

If a proposition is true, its denial is false; if a proposition is false, its denial is true. There are only two rows in this truth table since there are only two possibilities: a proposition is either true or false. A denial of a denied proposition (4th column) is logically equivalent to the original truth-value of the proposition as shown in the 2nd column.

Next, we show truth table descriptions of conjunction, disjunction, and implication. Each of these truth tables consists of four rows, since there are four possibilities given two values (true and false) and two propositions.

Conjunction

A conjunction is true if and only if both conjuncts are true; or, if a conjunction consists of more than two conjuncts, then it is true when each of its conjuncts is true. Otherwise, it is false. The first row depicts the meaning of true conjunction; the other three rows depict when a conjunction is false.

Rows	p	q	(p q)
1	T	T	T
2	T	F	F
3	F	T	F
4	F	F	F

Disjunction

An inclusive disjunction is false when both disjuncts are false. If the disjunction consists of more than two disjuncts, then it is false when each of the disjuncts is false. Otherwise, the disjunction is true as seen in rows1-3 of the last column.

Rows	p	q	(p ∨ q)
1	T	T	T
2	T	F	T
3	F	T	T
4	F	F	F

The fourth row depicts the meaning of a false disjunction. The first three rows, where both disjuncts and one or the other is true, complete the full meaning of inclusive disjunction.

Implication

One combination of values is fatal to an implication: true antecedent, false consequent. Otherwise, an implication is true as defined in this truth table.

Rows	p	q	(p < q)
1	T	T	T
2	T	F	F
3	F	T	T
4	F	F	T

To repeat: Row #2 displays the one combination of truth-values in which an implication is defined as false.

Truth Table Construction

The number of rows in a truth table depends on the number of distinct propositions of an argument. Each proposition is symbolized by a letter-variable or a "propositional variable."

For example, if an implication contains two distinct propositional variables, the truth table requires four rows. Since a single proposition can be true or false, a compound proposition of two simple propositions has four possibilities: (1) both can be true, (2) the first true and the second false, (3) the first false and the second true, and (4) both can be false. If a compound expression contains three distinct propositional variables, the number of rows is eight.

The formula for calculating the number of rows is $R = 2^n$, where **R** stands for rows, **2** stands for two truth-values (true and false), and **n** stands for the number of distinct variables. Thus for a compound of three distinct propositional variables (such as p, q, r), the number of rows is 2^3 or $(2 \times 2 \times 2) = 8$ rows.

Note, "p" and "p' " are not distinct variables; "p" and "q" are distinct, in our sense of the word.

Two practical concerns govern the arrangement of the truth-values in a truth table.

(1) Does the truth table contain all possible combinations of true and false? (2) Does the arrangement of truth-values, "T" and "F," result in a truth table that all can use without confusion.

With these concerns in mind, the construction of a truth table follows these steps:

Step1	Count the number of distinct variables in the expression to be analyzed.
Step2	Determine the number of rows required using the formula $R = 2^n$.
Step3	Assign 1st column (i) truth values as shown in the example below. (4 T's; 4 F's, assuming R = 8.)
Step4	Assign 2nd column (ii) truth-values as shown in the example below. (2 T's, 2 F's; etc.)
Step5	Assign 3rd column (iii) truth-values as shown in the example below. (T, F; T, F; etc.)

Given 3 distinct propositional variables and using the formula $R = 2^n$ will require a Truth Table of 8 rows as follows.

	(i)	(ii)	(iii)
	p	q	r
Row 1	T	T	T
Row 2	T	T	F
Row 3	T	F	T
Row 4	T	F	F
Row 5	F	T	T
Row 6	F	T	F
Row 7	F	F	T
Row 8	F	F	F

A more complex example follows. The expression is a disjunction where the first disjunct is a conjunction:

$$[(p \ q) \vee r)]$$

(Reminder. The brackets and parentheses are used as punctuation to indicate that the expression is a disjunction, i.e., the major logical connective is " $\vee$ ".)

First, enter the T's and F's for columns (i), (ii), (iii).

Second, enter truth-values in column (iv) for conjunction.

Third, enter truth-values for "r" once again in column (vi) to facilitate the last operation.

Fourth and last, determine the truth-values for disjunction under the major connective " $\vee$ " in column (v).

The truth-values of column (v) below are true, except for Rows 4, 6, and 8. Recall that an inclusive-or- disjunction is false if and only if each of its disjuncts is false. Truth table rows 4, 6, and 8 display this condition. The disjuncts (p g) and (r) in these rows are false.

	(i)	(ii)	(iii)	(iv)	(v)	(vi)
ROW	p	q	r	p q	∨	r
1	T	T	T	T	T	T
2	T	T	F	T	T	F
3	T	F	T	F	T	T
4	T	F	F	F	F*	F
5	F	T	T	F	T	T
6	F	T	F	F	F*	F
7	F	F	T	F	T	T
8	F	F	F	F	F*	F

To review. We assigned truth-values for three distinct variables in columns (i), (ii), and (iii) according to steps outlined earlier. We then assigned truth-values to each expression in columns (iv) and (v) according to the definitions of the appropriate logical connective -- working toward the major logical connective in column (v).

Now, suppose we wanted to display the relations between the following propositional expressions:

(1) (p < q)

(2) (pq ′)′

(3) (p′ ∨ q)

The first reads: if p then q; the second: it is not the case that p and not-q; the third: either not-p or q.

(Remember that parentheses are punctuation devices to indicate accurately the sense of the expression.)

There are 2 distinct propositional variables. Using $R = 2^n$, the number of rows is 4. The first column will contain 2 T's and 2 F's. The second column will consist of alternating T's and F's, for 4 rows as shown in the truth table below.

ROW	p	q	$(p < q)$	$(p\,q')'$	$(p' \vee q)$
1	T	T	T	T	T
2	T	F	F	F	F
3	F	T	T	T	T
4	F	F	T	T	T
	(i)	(ii)	(iii)	(iv)	(v)

The truth-values (T's and F's), beyond columns i and ii were assigned according to the definitions of the logical connectives. Notice columns (iii), (iv), and (v). The expressions have identical truth values in these columns – the expressions are logically equivalent. If one is true, the others are true also; and if any is false, the others are false as well. This truth table shows the relations between implication, conjunction, and disjunction as described previously in Chapter Four. The truth table above displays their interdefinability.

Symbolizing Implications

Students sometimes encounter difficulty in symbolizing more complicated implications or conditionals. The following list contains some of the more common expressions of implication.

p only if q	$p < q$
p thus q	$p < q$
p therefore q	$p < q$
p hence q	$p < q$
p if q	$q < p$
p since q	$q < p$
p because q	$q < p$
p for q	$q < p$

$$p \text{ when } q \qquad\qquad q < p$$

Other ways of expressing implications may not have the "If _, then_" formulation. For example, we use the word "implies" in "p implies q;" also, "q is implied by p."

Another example:

"Saving faith means belief in an understood proposition" is an implication made plain as, "If you possess saving faith, then you possess belief in the understood propositions of the Gospel." The key word is the verb, *means*. Thus, *x means y* is a formula for an implication: *if x, then y*.

The "if" introduces the antecedent of an implication, whereas "only if" introduces the consequent as in, "You are saved, only if you believe the Good News of the Bible."

Careful attention of the intended sense of a proposition is required in order to achieve its transformation into a correct propositional form.

Other Symbolizing Difficulties

Difficulties in symbolizing conjunctions may occur when the word "and" is absent, but implied. Other conjunction words used instead of "and" are: "but," "yet," "however," "although," "whereas," "nevertheless," and sometimes "plus," or, absent any of these words, merely a comma or a semicolon may imply the presence of a conjunction.

Is there a difference between "not both p and q" and "both not-p and not-q?" The first is the denial of a conjunction, $(pq)'$; the second is a conjunction of denials, $(p'\ q')$. To complicate matters, sometimes "and" in a proposition does not designate or denote a conjunction as defined in logic. For example, "1 and 1 is equal to 2," or "Peter and Paul were contemporaries" do not qualify as conjunctions in our sense.

Symbolizing disjunctions proves difficult when it is not clear which sense of *or* is the intended sense. Using the phrase "and/or" distinguishes the inclusive sense from the other senses. The phrase "but not both" signals the exclusive sense. The trouble is that these phrases are often implied, not explicitly stated. Of course, "$\vee$" stands for the inclusive sense; we have no symbol for the exclusive sense having decided that the inclusive sense serves our purposes well.

Nevertheless, suppose the exclusive sense is expressed as in "Either you are regenerate (r) or you are forever lost (l)." The expression of *or* as "one or the other, but not both" is symbolized as follows.

$$[(r \vee l) \ (r \ l)'].$$

Here is another minor difficulty involving disjunction.

"Neither p nor q" is not (p' $\vee$ q'). The correct symbolization is (p $\vee$ q)' -- a denial of the disjunction.

A less difficult case is the use of "unless" in "Unless you study logic, you will believe propaganda." This proposition means "Either you study logic, or you'll believe propaganda."

Again, careful attention is required to achieve the correct transformation of the intended sense of a propositional form.

Truth Table Application

Next, we provide an example that applies truth table methods. It is an exercise from Gordon Clark's *Logic*, modified slightly. Our purpose is not only to show the advantages of symbolizing propositions, but also to indicate how truth tables may assist understanding relations among propositions.

Either D.L. Moody was a successful evangelist or Billy Sunday was a failure. If Billy Sunday was not a failure, Billy Graham is. Either D.L. Moody was not a [successful evangelist] or Billy Graham is not [a failure]. If Billy Sunday was a failure, then Billy Graham is not. (*Logic*, HC ed., p. 106).

m stands for "Moody was a successful evangelist;"

s stands for "Sunday was a failure;"

g stands for "Graham is a failure."

m $\vee$ s	Either Moody was a successful evangelist or Billy Sunday was a failure.
s' < g	If Sunday was not a failure, then Graham is a failure.
m' $\vee$ g'	Either Moody was not a successful evangelist or Graham is not a failure.
s < g'	If Sunday was a failure, then Graham is not a failure.

Truth-Table Analysis

	m	s	g	m∨s	s′<g	m′∨g′	s<g′
1	T	T	T	T	T	F	F
2**	T	T	F	T	T	T	T**
3	T	F	T	T	T	F	T
4	T	F	F	T	F	T	T
5	F	T	T	T	T	T	F
6**	F	T	F	T	T	T	T**
7	F	F	T	F	T	T	T
8	F	F	F	F	F	T	T
	(i)	(ii)	(iii)	(iv)	(v)	(vi)	(vii)

**Rows 2 and 6 are the only ones that have values of true for the four compound expressions in columns (iv) through (vii).

Focus on rows 2 and 6, where all of the compound propositions are true. Examine the truth-values of the propositional variables m, s, and g in columns (i), (ii) and (iii), respectively. These two rows show true for all of the compound propositions. Notice the contradictory values for m in column (i), Rows 2 and 6; so nothing can be said about m (Moody), one way or another. However, s is true in Rows 2 and 6, and g is false in the same rows. So it is true that Sunday was a failure, but false that Graham is a failure, according to this truth table analysis.

Since this truth table is not an analysis of an argument, there is no question of the validity of an argument. The truth table provides an analysis of simple propositions assuming the truth of the compound propositions.

Modus Ponens Revisited

Suppose we submit Modus Ponens to truth table analysis. Formulated as a truth-function expression where the conjunction of the premises is the antecedent of an implication and the conclusion is the consequent, modus ponens as a truth function has this form:

$$[(p < q) (p)] < (q)$$

Will a truth table analysis reveal that Modus Ponens is a valid argument form?

			Premise1	Premise2	∴	Conclusion
	p	q	p < q	p	<	q
1	T	T	T	T	T	T
2	T	F	F	T	T	F
3	F	T	T	F	T	T
4	F	F	T	F	T	F
	(i)	(ii)	(iii)	(iv)	(v)	(vi)

Columns (iv) and (vi) are identical to columns (i) and (ii), respectively, being the identical variables. If the argument were invalid, one would expect to find at least one row in which the premises are both true and the conclusion false. Inspection of Rows 2 and 4 shows the conclusion "q" is false, but in both instances, one of the premises is also false. Only in Row 1 are the premises true and the conclusion true also. In a valid argument form, it is impossible for the premises to be true and the conclusion false. Thus, Modus Ponens proves valid by truth table methods.

The truth table reveals all T's under the major logical connective, "<" of column (v). Column (v), the "therefore" column, represents the truth values of the expression: [(p < q) (p), ∴ (q)]. Under all possible assignments of T's and F's to the distinct variables of this valid argument form, the result reveals all T's under the major logical connective, an additional confirmation that Modus Ponens is a valid argument form.

Let us now contrast this argument form with the associated fallacy.

Fallacy of Affirming the Consequent Revisited

Symbolizing the fallacy as an implication we have:

[(p < q) (q)] < (p)

As with the previous treatment of modus ponens, the last "<" is the major logical connective. The premises are a conjunction within the brackets and constitute the antecedent of the implication. "(p)," is the conclusion or the consequent of the implication.

	p	q	Premise1 p < q	Premise2 q	∴ <	Conclusion p
1	T	T	T	T	T	T
2	T	F	F	F	T	T
3	F	T	T	T	F	F
4	F	F	T	F	T	F
	(i)	(ii)	(iii)	(iv)	(v)	(vi)

The truth-values of columns (ii) and (iv) are identical; columns (i) and (vi) are also identical. Again, if the argument were invalid, one would expect to find at least one row in which both of the premises are true and the conclusion false. Inspection of Row 3 shows that both of the premises are true and the conclusion false. Column (v), the "∴" column, represents the truth values of the expression, [(p < q) (q), ∴ (p)]. The third row shows false under the major logical connective (<) precisely at the row that shows true premises and a false conclusion. Therefore, the argument form is invalid, as we knew it to be.

Do not be confused by the truth-values of Row 1 where the premises are true and the conclusion is true also. This only indicates the possibility of an invalid argument with true propositions. In a valid argument form, true premises imply a true conclusion -- always. "Always" means in each and every row of a truth table. The only "F" in column (v), Row 3, confirms that we are in the presence of an implication with true premises and a false conclusion. Thus, the fallacy of affirming the consequent proves to be an invalid argument form by truth table methods.

Summary

Truth tables are schemata for analyzing the relations between different propositions, simple or compound. In this chapter, the meanings of the logical connectives for true and false propositions, conjunction, disjunction, and implication were elucidated using truth table methods. Thereafter, we set down instructions for constructing truth tables.

Applications followed using various examples.

Finally, two argument forms, one valid and one invalid, were analyzed using truth tables. The results demonstrated that with a valid argument form, expressed as an implication, no single row shows true premises and a false conclusion. On the other hand, the invalid argument form, expressed as an implication, revealed a row with true premises and a false conclusion. As a heuristic method, truth table analysis not only confirms validity and invalidity of argument forms, but also provides a practical method for illustrating both.

Review

Do a truth-table analysis of the following four compound propositions.

Either the birds are singing or the baby is crying. If the baby is not crying, then the wind is blowing. Either the birds are not singing or the wind is not blowing. [If the baby is crying, then the wind is not blowing.]

Questions to answer: Are the birds singing? Is the baby crying? Is the wind blowing? (Gordon H. Clark. *Logic*, HC ed., p. 106; proposition in brackets added).

S = the birds are singing

C = the baby is crying

B = the wind is blowing.

	S	C	B	S∨C	C′<B	S′∨B′	C<B′
1	T	T	T				
2	T	T	F				
3	T	F	T				

	(i)	(ii)	(iii)	(iv)	(v)	(vi)	(vii)
4	T	F	F				
5	F	T	T				
6	F	T	F				
7	F	F	T				
8	F	F	F				

Exercise 6.1: Truth Table - Functions

Part A Instructions: Match the truth table values in the columns a through g with the correct Forms 1 through 7.

X	Y	a	b	c	d	e	f	g
T	T	T	T	F	F	T	F	F
T	F	F	F	T	T	T	F	F
F	T	T	F	T	F	T	F	T
F	F	T	F	T	F	F	T	T

	FORMS	CHOICE
1	conjunction	
2	disjunction	
3	implication	
4	contradiction of conjunction	
5	contradiction of disjunction	
6	contradiction of implication	

7	contradiction of variable X	

Part B Instructions: Match the truth table values in the columns a through g with the expressions 1-10.

P	Q	a	b	c	d	e	f	g
T	T	T	F	F	T	T	T	F
T	F	T	F	T	F	F	T	F
F	T	T	F	T	T	F	F	F
F	F	T	F	T	T	F	F	T

	EXPRESSIONS	CHOICES
1	$(p \vee q)'$	
2	$(pp')'$	
3	$(p \vee p')'$	
4	$(pq)'$	
5	$(p' \vee q)$	
6	$(pq')'$	
7	$(p' \vee q')$	
8	$(p' \vee q')'$	
9	$(p < p')'$	
10	$(p' \vee p')'$	

Exercise 6.2: Truth Table Example

Instructions: Do a truth table analysis of the following.

Hawk is good in either science or theology, but not both. Moreover, either he is good at logic or bad at theology. If he is not good in science, he is bad at theology. If he is bad at theology, he is good at logic.

What do these four premises imply?

1	Hawk is good in either science or theology, but not both.	$(s \vee t)(s\ t)'$
2	Hawk is good at logic or bad at theology.	$l \vee t'$
3	If he is not good in science, he is bad at theology.	$s' < t'$
4	If he is bad at theology, he is good at logic.	$t' < l$

	s	l	t	$(s \vee t)(s\ t)'$	$l \vee t'$	$s' < t'$	$t' < l$
1	T	T	T				
2	T	T	F				
3	T	F	T				
4	T	F	F				
5	F	T	T				
6	F	T	F				
7	F	F	T				
8	F	F	F				
	i	ii	iii	iv	v	vi	vii

7 INFORMAL FALLACIES

A fallacy is a blunder in reasoning. It is "false" reasoning with illogical or misleading argument. *Reasoning* means drawing inferences or conclusions from known or assumed facts or premises. The premises and conclusions of arguments should qualify as propositions, i.e., the meanings of declarative sentences that possess the essential characteristic of being either true or false. Recall that an argument is a series of connected declarative sentences (premises) in support of another statement (conclusion) or a position. In other words, a fallacy consists of invalid or unwarranted inference of a conclusion from premises, some of which may not qualify as propositions.

Commands, exhortations, or exclamations, for instance, do not possess the quality of truth or falsity and must be reworded into propositions if they are to serve as either premises or conclusions.

Fallacies Classified

Fallacies of form render arguments invalid irrespective of the content of the argument or the truth or falsity of its propositions with the following qualification. If the form of an argument allows an inference of a false conclusion from all true premises, then we know the argument to be invalid, for a valid argument will never result in the deduction of a false conclusion from true premises. Indeed, if it so happens that the conclusion of a particular argument is known to be false and the argument is valid, then we know that at least one of the premises is false as well.

Informal fallacies, unlike formal fallacies, are not fallacies of form. Extralogical or emotional appeals usually constitute one of the sources of persuasion. In other cases, informal fallacies are deceptive pieces of "bad" English or mistakes due to ambiguity or vagueness of a term or phrase, or an entire sentence. In any case, the pretense of logical relevance, we could say, is the source of fallacy. Informal fallacy is counterfeit argument, i.e., a type of argument that appears to be sound but which proves on examination not to be.

Informal Fallacies

The language of informal fallacies may present the appearance or structure of a deductive argument with premises *in-support-of* a conclusion. However, herein is the possibility of error -- if one interprets the *in-support-of* as a necessary inference relation. While there is a relation between premises and conclusion in such "arguments," the relation is a psychological one consisting, in many instances, of emotional appeals to agree with or accept a conclusion.

Not a few individuals use informal fallacies to create a special effect in the listener conducive to agreement with a conclusion. The art of using language to persuade acceptance of a conclusion by appeal to feelings of attraction or aversion to an object or event has a long history. Many commercials make use of attraction and/or aversion for things or circumstances to persuade customers to avoid something by buying a product or to attain an attractive status by using a product. One should not ignore the context in determining whether a piece of language is nothing more than counterfeit argument.

Informal fallacy classifications abound. Perhaps the simplest consists of two categories of the most common types: (1) fallacies of irrelevant conclusion; and (2) fallacies of ambiguity and vagueness.

Fallacies of Relevance

Fallacies of irrelevant conclusion are those for which the premises are not relevant to the truth of the conclusion. With such, the label *non sequitur,* meaning literally that the conclusion does not follow from the premises is often used. With these fallacies the premises are incapable of establishing the conclusion logically because they are irrelevant to the conclusion. Some of the more common informal fallacies have retained their Latin names.

Table 7.1 Fallacies of Relevance

Argumentum ad hominem-abusive	AH	When irrelevancies of character, circumstances, the beliefs or prejudices of the person used as a ploy to reject a position or conclusion.
Argumentum ad baculum	AB	When one appeals to force or the threat of force instead of reason to cause acceptance of a conclusion.
Argumentum ad misericordiam	AM	When one appeals to pity instead of sound reasoning to gain acceptance of a conclusion.
Argumentum ad populum	AP	When one attempts to gain popular assent to a conclusion by arousing the feelings and enthusiasms of the multitude.
		Appeals that one should accept a conclusion since everyone else or most people have accepted it.
Argumentum ad verecundiam	AV	When instead of sound argument appeals to the feeling of respect people may have for the famous to win assent to a conclusion.
Argumentum ad ignorantiam	AI	Whenever argued that a proposition is true solely on the basis that it has not been proved false, or that it is false

		because it has not been proved true.
False Cause	FC	Infers that because one event follows another, the first event caused the second. (*post hoc ergo propter hoc* or "after this, therefore because of this")
False Dilemma	FD	Calls for a conclusion based on assumption that only two options are possible, when more than two are possible or the two are not mutually exclusive.
Accident	A	When an accidental or irrelevant factor treated as the essential point in argument.
Hasty Generalization	HG	In argument considers only exceptional or too few cases and generalizes universally to a rule that fits them alone.
Circular Reasoning	CR	Assumes as a premise for an argument the very conclusion that is intended to be proved. (*petitio principii* or "begging the question")
Complex Question	CQ	In argument treats a plurality of questions as if it were a simple one demanding a single answer.

As opposed to reasoned exchange, consider the following dialogue, replete with informal fallacies.

Table 7.2 Dialogue in Fallacies

She	"You're just like your father--lazy and sloppy!"	AH
He	"You wouldn't talk that way in front of my Dad!"	AB
She	"Maybe not, but I get no help from you; after 40 hours of hard work, I do all, I mean all the house cleaning and cooking while you watch TV?"	AM
He	"All women who want both career and marriage seem to feel very happy about doing both! That's what all successful women say."	AP

She	"Would Mr. Rogers, your hero, hold the opinions you have about marriages and careers?"	AV
He	"Mr. Rogers has never argued that career and marriage are incompatible for women. Therefore, he must believe that they are compatible."	AI
She	"Don't talk to me about Mr. Rogers. The last time you brought him into our discussion, we had a terrible fight!"	FC
He	"I didn't bring Rogers into our discussion, you did! You either like him or you don't; I see you don't!"	FD
She	"It's not a question of liking Rogers or not. It's the way you use what he says. One should never take what other people say out of context, as you do with Mr. Rogers."	A
He	"This is the third time you have accused me of using what Mr. Rogers' says. When you run out of good arguments, you always say this about me."	HG
She	"This is just like you! You conclude that you are innocent of any wrong-doing because you are innocent of any wrong-doing!"	CR
He	"When will you stop hassling me?"	CQ

A counterfeit-deductive argument may employ more than one fallacy and fit into more than one. Even with exhaustive information about the context, one may find it difficult, if not impossible, to classify a particular counterfeit argument into one and only one type. Language serves multiple purposes, and those purposes are themselves in the service of hidden agendas or motives. In cases where there exists the possibility of classifying a counterfeit argument into more than one known category, we can agree that it is one or the other, and possibly both. This should not preclude effort to classify them, however, based on the defining characteristics of known categories.

Fallacies of Ambiguity

Fallacies of ambiguity occur in formulations of argument that use ambiguous words or phrases. This is a smaller class of fallacies that include the fallacies of equivocation, amphibology, accent, composition, and division.

Table 7.3: Fallacies of Ambiguity

equivocation	EQU	Confuses the different meanings a single word or phrase may have.
amphibology	AMP	Meaning is unclear because of the loose or awkward way in which the words combined.
accent	ACC	Words or phrases emphasized or stressed producing different meanings from the original.
composition	COM	Reasoning from properties of the part to properties of the whole itself.
division	DIV	Reasoning that what is true of a whole is true of each of the whole's parts.

It is not difficult to come up with examples of each of the above. Some uses are a mere play on words as in "Good steaks are rare these days, so don't order yours well-done" where the equivocation turns on the meanings of "rare." More serious perhaps, is this one:

"The end of a thing is its perfection; death is the end of life. Therefore, death is the perfection of life." (EQU) (Examine the meanings of "end.")

In this next example, the ambiguity lies in the structure or syntax of the sentence:

"Leaking badly manned by a starved and thirsty crew one infirmity after another overtakes the little ship." (AMP) Obviously, the phrase "manned … crew" and perhaps other words need to be revised to achieve an unambiguous meaning.

The statement, "We should not speak ill of our friends." when quoted as, "We should not speak ill of OUR FRIENDS" (ACC) stresses words not emphasized in the original, thereby conveying a different meaning(s) from the original.

Composition and division are closely related. For example, if someone argues that based on the properties of the elements of NaCl, the compound must be highly toxic (COM), one might suspect that the person does not know the compound is table salt. On the other hand, if someone argued that since salt possesses a class of salutary properties; therefore, the salt's elements (sodium and chloride) must be salutary, instruction in chemistry and perhaps more, may be required.

Avoiding Informal Fallacies

Context is important in determining when to label something as informal fallacy. For example, when there is no attempt to disguise an emotional appeal as a necessary inference, there may be no point in accusing someone of using an informal fallacy. On the other hand, when all logical appeals have failed to convince a perverse arguer who knowingly and willfully disregards truth for error, what else remains but *ad hominem* (not the abusive variety)? There are occasions where the use of blunt, even *ad baculum* language may be the only alternative; for example, as when a police officer is confronted by an armed felon.

Ad hominem must not be confused with the abusive kind. *Ad hominem* is a form of argument that assumes the propositions of another for the sake of deducing contradictions or conclusions unacceptable to the person holding the position.

Consider too that there are special circumstances where it is quite appropriate to direct a complex question to another. For example. "Where did you hide the body?" or "Do you know the penalty for perjury?" are questions that are not classified as instances of informal fallacy, once the groundwork has been established for their use. Again. Context is important in assessing the use of language.

What can one do to avoid informal fallacy? It should be evident that telling someone that he or she is engaging in *ad hominem abusive* reasoning may not have the desired effect of causing the person to pause and reflect on his or her thinking. The person may not know what you mean by *ad hominem*, or *informal fallacy*. Nevertheless, identification of the counterfeit argument by appropriate label is an important first step. A second step requires clear definitions of ambiguous or vague terms. In a third step one may construct a counterexample, analogous in every respect with the informal fallacy in which the premises are obviously true and the conclusion obviously false.

For example, suppose someone argues:

"If President Kennedy was assassinated, then he is dead. Now, all acknowledge that he is indeed dead. Therefore, President Kennedy was assassinated."

This argument is formally fallacious, being guilty of the Fallacy of Affirming the Consequent. However, another way of demonstrating the fallacy, perhaps more effective than using formal methods, would be to offer a counterargument that is obviously fallacious.

Constructing a counterargument to make explicit fallacious reasoning requires that (1) the propositions be of the same form as the original, (2) the format be identical to the original, and (3) true premises and obviously false conclusion.

A counter argument example follows.

"You may just as well argue that if President Johnson was assassinated, then he is dead. President Johnson is dead. Therefore, President Johnson was assassinated."

Obviously, the conclusion of the counterargument does not follow from the true premises. Similarly, the conclusion of the previous argument is not necessitated by its premises.

Definitions

Among the best ways to avoid vagueness or ambiguity in the language of argument is to define key terms clearly. Good definitions of terms in unambiguous language will prevent much confusion and controversy. Moreover, it is unwise to assume that different users always have the same meaning when using the same word or phrase.

To define a term or phrase clearly means to state univocally what it means or signifies.

Definition, according to purpose yields a number of classes of definition described in Table 7.4 below.

Table: 7.4 Definitions by Purpose

TYPES	PURPOSES	EXAMPLES
Lexical	To report meaning of a term to increase vocabulary or	Unicorn is "an animal-like horse

	eliminating ambiguity; assessed true or false. (real or reportive definition)	having a single straight horn projecting from its forehead."
Stipulative	To introduce new term (or a new use for old one) to increase vocabulary; proposal to use a word or phrase in a certain way; includes abbreviations or acronyms; not assessed as true or false. (nominal or verbal definition)	By *hermeneut*, I mean "one who is obsessed with one kind of interpretation – one's own."
Precising	To reduce vagueness of term beyond lexical but faithful to established usage; applies to borderline cases; assessed partially true or false.	In a correlation study of police height and job injuries, *short* means "a height of less than 5 foot 6."
Theoretical	To provide characterization of the objects to which applied, to increase and systematize knowledge, to solve theoretical issues, takes account of previous usage; assessed by status of a theory. (analytic definition)	*Justice* may be defined as "getting what one is due."
Persuasive	To influence or change attitudes by the emotive or evaluative use of language; assessed as successful or not in changing attitudes. (rhetorical definition)	Television news reporters constitute an unelected "kakistocracy" meaning "government by the worst available citizens."

In addition, definitions may be classified as either denotative or designative.

Definitions are denotative when the portion of the statement that does the defining, *the definiens*, refers to a set of objects or events to which the term applies correctly. For example, one could define "valid argument form" by naming each one: modus ponens, modus tollens, disjunctive syllogism, etc.

While denotative definitions name the members or objects of a term or class, a designative definition's *definiens* consists of the essential characteristics or the necessary and sufficient attributes of the *definiendum*, the term defined.

Designative definitions, in turn, divide into synonymous and analytic types. Synonymous definitions have not only the same designation but also the same denotation (if any). Analytic definitions not only designate, but provide an analysis of the definiendum in the definiens.

Analytic definitions play an important role in research and philosophical discussions.

The following table describes analytic types with an example for each.

Table 7.5: Definitions by Method

TYPES	ANALYTIC	EXAMPLE
Genus & Difference	Subsumes the definiendum as species under its genus; specifies difference between it and other species in the genus.	*Triangle* =df "a polygon having three sides." (Also known as connotative definition.)
Genetic	Definiens describes the origin or development of the definiendum.	*Niece* =df "the daughter of one's sister or brother."
Causal	Definiens provides the cause(s) of the definiendum.	*Red Shift* =df "the systematic movement toward longer wave lengths in the spectra of light caused by the star moving away."
Functional	Definiens describes purpose(s) or function(s) of the definiendum.	*Ornament* =df "anything serving to adorn, decorate, or embellish."

Analogical	Definiens describes similarities and differences of two or more things one of which is the definiendum.	*Lyre* =df "a small stringed instrument similar to a harp used by the ancient Greeks to accompany singers and reciters."
Antonymous	Definiens describes definiendum in terms of opposition between the two.	*Fair-minded* =df "free from bias or prejudice."
Operational	Definiens describes set of procedures, or public and repeatable steps or methods, for correct application of definiendum.	*Acid* =df "a substance that will turn blue litmus paper red when brought into contact with it."

Some useful questions to keep in mind when evaluating definitions follow.

Does the definition avoid circularity, i.e., using the same word in the definiens that is being defined?

Does the definition avoid the use of negative terms in the definiens?

Is the definition either too narrow, or too broad, i.e., either excluding too much or including too much?

Does the definition avoid obscure or figurative language, vague terms, or emotively loaded terminology?

Does the definition serve the purpose for which it was intended?

Gordon Clark remarks on the necessity for good definitions this way:

"Strict definitions and strict adherence to them are essential to intelligible discussion. If one contender has one idea in mind – or perhaps no clear idea at all, while the other party to the debate entertains a different notion, or is equally vague – the result of the conversation is bound to be complete confusion." (*God and Evil*, p. 16)

Summary

Informal fallacies are counterfeit arguments. Counterfeit argument is a sub-class of a larger class known as propaganda or language used to create special effects. It should be clear that when the connection between premises and conclusion in a given context is obviously psychological, masquerading as a necessary inference, we are in the presence of counterfeit argument – informal fallacy.

In this chapter two classes of informal fallacies were described: fallacies of relevance and fallacies of ambiguity. Fallacies of relevance, as the label suggests, are those in which the premises are not logically relevant to the truth of the conclusion. Some of the more common informal fallacies have retained their Latin names. Others may not have received either a Latin or English label, being less familiar. With these, the label *non sequitur*, meaning that the conclusion does not follow from the premises, is often used. Fallacies of ambiguity occur in formulations of argument that use ambiguous words or phrases. This is a smaller class that includes the fallacies of equivocation, amphibology, accent, composition, and division.

To avoid informal fallacy, it can be effective to ask for a clear definition of key terms. Articulating a clear understanding of crucial terms can serve to avoid the vagueness or ambiguity that feeds controversy based on misunderstanding or misinterpreted language. Nevertheless, even with all precautions, there is no certain way to avoid counterfeit arguments. The logical task requires practice, vigilance, and clear, precise language.

Review

Suppose the following definition of *definition*.

Definition is a statement that captures the meaning, use, function, and essence of a concept, term or phrase.

1. Does it fail the requirements for adequate definition listed previously in this chapter?

2. Would you classify the definition above as a denotative or connotative definition? Why?

3. Does the definiens use terms that require definition?

4. In what context would this definition be essential to intelligible discussion?

5. Compare the above definition with your dictionary definition. How do the two differ?

Exercise 7.1 True/False Statements

Instructions: Which of the following is true and which is false? If false, how could it be reworded to qualify as a true statement?

ITEMS	STATEMENTS	T/F
1	Fallacies are classified as either formal or informal.	
2	Informal Fallacies are fallacies of form rather than content.	
3	Argumentum Ad Baculum is classified as a Fallacy of Relevance.	
4	The Fallacy of Accident occurs when one assumes as a premise the conclusion intended to be proved.	
5	The Fallacy of False Dilemma poses two and only two alternatives when there are more than two choices.	
6	Fallacies of Relevance are a smaller class than Fallacies of Ambiguity.	
7	Fallacies of Ambiguity include two that speak of the relation between the attributes of a part or parts and the whole.	
8	*Amphibology* is a Fallacy of Relevance.	
9	*Ad hominem* is a form of argument that deduces conclusions unacceptable to another person's premises.	
10	Lexical Definition introduces a new term or new use for an old term.	
11	The purpose of a Precising Definition is the reduction or elimination of vague terminology.	
12	Synonymous definitions have the same connotation and denotation if any.	

13	*Definiens* designates the term or phrase to be defined.	
14	That portion of a definition that provides the meaning of a term is called the *definiendum*.	
15	One way to avoid counterfeit argument is by means of clear and precise definitions of vague or ambiguous terminology.	

Exercise 7.2 Fallacies Defined

Instructions: Fill in the box next to each item with the letter of the most correct answer. If no correct answer is listed, choose " p " None of the Above.

a	accent	i	amphibology
b	ad baculum	j	circular reasoning
c	ad hominem (abusive)	k	complex question
d	ad ignorantiam	l	composition
e	ad misericordiam	m	division
f	ad populum	n	post hoc
g	ad verecundiam	o	false dilemma
h	equivocation	p	None of the Above

ITEMS	STATEMENTS	
1	When one appeals to force or threat of force to cause acceptance of a conclusion.	
2	When instead of trying to disprove the truth of what is asserted, one attacks the person's situation, beliefs, or character.	

3	Whenever it is argued that a proposition is true (false) simply on the basis that it has not been proved false (true).	
4	The attempt to win popular assent to a conclusion by arousing the feelings and enthusiasms of the multitude, or appealing to popular opinion.	
5	An appeal to the feeling of respect people have for the famous to win assent to a conclusion.	
6	When one argues that another must choose one of two choices without having proven that the choices are mutually exclusive.	
7	When one considers only exceptional cases and generalizes to a rule that fits them alone.	
8	When one assumes as a premise for an argument the very conclusion one intends to prove.	
9	When pity is appealed to for the sake of getting a conclusion accepted.	
10	When we confuse the different meanings a single word or phrase may have.	
11	When a statement's meaning is unclear because of the loose way in which its words are combined.	
12	When words or phrases of a statement are emphasized or stressed producing a different meaning from the original.	
13	When one reasons from the properties of the parts of a whole to the properties of the whole itself.	
14	Assuming without proof that a prior event explains or is the cause of a subsequent event.	
15	When one argues fallaciously that what is true of a whole must be true of each of its parts.	

Exercise 7.3 Definitions

Instructions: Fill in the blank(s) in each item with the letter of the most correct answer. If no correct answer is listed, choose "n " None of the Above.

a	analytic	h	ostensive
b	denotative	i	persuasive
c	designative	j	precising
d	genetic	k	stipulative
e	genus & difference	l	synonymous
f	lexical	m	theoretical
g	operational	n	None of the Above

STATEMENTS
1. A definition that reports the conventional meaning of a term is known as a(n) _____ definition.
2. Definitions that introduce a term either having no previous meaning or assigning a new one are said to be _____ .
3. If a definition gives a more precise meaning to a term, it is call a(n) _____ definition.
4. Definitions given for the purpose of solving theoretical problems (among other matters) are called. _____ .
5. _____ definitions are attempts to change attitudes toward either favorable or unfavorable connotations or denotations.
6. Definitions according to method are classified as _____ or _____ .
7. A definition that lists the members of the term/class being defined is known as _____ .
8. A definition whose definiendum and definiens are exact equivalents in every respect are said to be _____ .
9. _____ definition is a designative one in which the definiens provides an analysis of the meaning of the definiendum.
10. A statement of the way in which members of a subclass differ from other members of the general class is a definition by _____ .

11. _____ definition describes the origin or development of the class being defined.
12. _____ definition specifies a set of procedures for determining whether a term can be correctly applied.

8 GLOSSARY

The number(s) in parentheses following each description refers to the chapter number(s). See the outline at the beginning of each chapter for more information.

A Form. This form of a standard proposition states that All a is b, or A(ab). (2)

affirmative quality. A form that does not distribute its predicate term. (2)

affirming the consequent. A fallacy, resulting when one asserts the consequent of an implication in order to infer the antecedent as its conclusion. (5, 6)

argument. A series of connected reasons in support of a position or a conclusion. (1)

axiom. A first principle or premise. (4)

conclusion. The proposition deduced from a previous proposition or set of propositions. (1)

contradiction. Two propositions that cannot both be false together and cannot both be true together. (1, 3)

contraposition. An immediate inference that consists in contradicting both subject and predicate terms, then interchanging them. Valid for A and O, but not for I. E by limitation. (3)

contraries. Two propositions that cannot be both true together, but could be both false. (3)

conversion. The interchange of the subject and predicate of a proposition. Valid for E and I but not for O, and Form A *per accidens*, or by limitation. (3)

copula. The present tense of the verb to be; connects the subject and predicate. (2, 3)

deduction. A process of reasoning in which the conclusion follows necessarily from the premises presented. (4)

definiendum. The word or phrase subject to definition. (7)

definiens. That portion of a definition that explains or describes the word or phrase defined. (7)

definitions by method. Genus & difference, genetic, causal, functional, analogical, antonymous, and operational are members of the class of definitions according to the methodology used to define a term or phrase. (7)

definitions by purpose. Lexical, stipulative, precising, theoretical, and persuasive are included in the class of definitions according to the specific purpose intended. (7)

denying the antecedent. A formal fallacy that results when one denies the antecedent of an implication in order to infer the denial of the consequent as conclusion. (5)

diagrams. Representations that employ Euler circles in order to demonstrate validity of an inference or validity of a deductive argument; known in logic as Venn Diagrams. (4)

dilemma. An argument form, valid when criteria of valid implications and complete disjunction of the premises are met. Symbolized as $[(a < b) \ (c < d) \ (a \lor c)] < (b \lor d)$. (5)

disjunctive hypothetical syllogism. Symbolically: Either a or b, not-a; therefore, b. (4)

distribution. A distributed term in a proposition is one modified by All, or No. (2)

E Form. The form of a standard proposition that states that No a is b, or E(ab). (2)

enthymeme. An argument in which one or more of the propositions is suppressed or taken for granted. (4)

fallacy. A mistake or blunder in reasoning. (5, 7)

fallacy of ambiguity. Formulation of an argument in ambiguous words or phrases. (7)

fallacy of relevance. An argument in which the premises are not relevant to the truth of the conclusion. (7)

figure in a syllogism. The relative position of the middle term in the premises; there are 4 positions or 4 figures. (4)

form. The subject and predicate arrangement in a proposition. There are four forms: All a is b; No a is b; Some a is b; and Some a is not b. (2)

formal property of forms. There are three properties shared by the four forms: distribution, quantity, and quality. (2)

frame. Form of a syllogism that is determined by the different positions of the terms in the premises and conclusion, the mood and figure of a syllogism. (4)

grammatical subject. Syntactic unit of a sentence that refers to one performing an action or being in the state expressed by the predicate; the subject of the verb is the grammatical subject. (2)

I Form. A standard form proposition: Some a is b, or I(ab). (2)

immediate inference. An argument consisting of one premise and a conclusion. (3)

implication. The relation between two propositions in virtue of which one is logically deducible from the other. (3)

indicator words. Words or phrases that introduce or otherwise indicate the presence of premises and conclusions of an argument. Premise Indicator Words and Conclusion Indicator Words. (1)

inference. The forming of a conclusion from premises by logical methods. (1, 2)

informal fallacy. Reasoning with illogical or misleading argument; a counterfeit of necessary inference. (7)

invalid inference. That which has occurred when the conclusion of an argument did not follow logically from premises such that the argument fails one of the rules for validity. (3, 6)

law of contradiction. This law states that the same attribute cannot at the same time belong and not belong to the same subject and in the same respect. Symbolized: Not both a and not-a; or (aa')'. (1, 5)

law of excluded middle. This law states that everything must either be or not be. Symbolized: a or not-a; or (a ∨ a'). (1, 5)

law of identity. This law states: If any proposition is true, then it is true. Symbolized: (a < a). (1, 5)

logic. The science of necessary inference; the systematic study of valid reasoning. (1), *passim*.

logical connective. The part that joins simple propositions to form compound propositions such as "and," "or," "not," and "implies" each symbolized. (6)

logical subject. Thoughts and utterances are about something; that something is the logical subject. The subject causing the action is the real or logical subject, what the statement is about. (2)

major premise. The premise that contains the major term. (4)

major term. Predicate of the conclusion of a syllogism or an inference. (4)

mediate inference. See "syllogism." (4)

middle term. The term that one finds in each of the premises of a syllogism, but not in the conclusion. (4)

minor premise. The premise that contains the minor term. (4)

minor term. The subject of the conclusion of a syllogism or an inference. (4)

modus ponens. Valid formal argument form; "a way of constructing;" symbolically: "If p, then q; p; therefore, q". (5, 6)

modus tollens. Valid formal argument form; "a way of destroying;" symbolically: "If p, then q; not-q; therefore, not-p." (4, 5)

mood. A label combining 3 of the propositional forms (A, E, I, or O) standing for a syllogism. First letter designates the major premise. Second letter, the minor premise, Third letter, the conclusion. (4)

necessary inference. When a conclusion follows logically, strictly, from premises. (1)

negation. The denial of a true proposition is false. Denial of a false proposition is true. A proposition is either true or false. (6)

negative quality. A form that distributes its predicate. (2)

nonstandard categorical proposition. A categorical proposition other than A, E, I, or O. (2, 4)

nonstandard syllogism. A syllogism that contains more than 3 standard terms or is expressed as an enthymeme. (4)

O Form. The form of a standard proposition that states that Some a is not b, or O(ab). (2)

obversion. A valid immediate inference; the replacement of one form by another in which the quality of the first is changed and the predicate replaced by its contradictory or complement. (3)

parameter. A word or phrase in both the subject and predicate used to translate nonstandard propositions to standard forms. (2)

particular quantity. Refers to a form that does not distribute its subject. (2)

per accidens. Conversion of A form to I form. (3)

premise. The proposition of an argument from which a conclusion is drawn, a reason intended to support a conclusion. (1)

proposition. A form of words in which the predicate is affirmed or denied of the subject, the meaning expressed by a declarative sentence. (1)

quality. The two types are affirmative and negative; A and I forms have affirmative quality. The E and O forms have negative quality. (2)

quantity. The two types are universal and particular; A and E forms have universal quantity. The I and O forms have particular quantity. (2)

reductio ad absurdum. Also reductio ad impossible. Deducing by valid inference a conclusion you know to be false. (4)

reflexive. A relationship that holds between one of its objects and the object itself. (3)

sorites. An argument consisting of a chain of propositions in which the predicate of each is the subject of the next, the conclusion consisting of the first subject and the last predicate. (4)

sound. A quality of valid deductive arguments when all of the propositions are true. (1)

square of opposition. A scheme for displaying the four relationships of contrariety, subcontrariety, subalternation, and contradiction among the forms A, E, I, and O. (3)

subalterns. Refers to the opposition between two propositions both alike in quality; the propositions may both be true together or both false together. (3)

subcontraries. Refers to two propositions (I and O) that cannot both be false together, but could both be true. (3)

syllogism. An argument of three propositions, two premises and a conclusion, with the conclusion's subject term in one of the premises, the predicate of the conclusion in the other premise, and a third term found in both premises only. (4)

symmetrical. Refers to a relationship which, if it holds between two objects, a and b, also holds between b and a. (3)

theorem. A proposition deduced from an axiom and/or other theorems. (4)

transitive. Refers to a relationship which, if it holds for a and b, and also holds for b and c, holds as well between a and c. (3)

transitive hypothetical syllogism (See "transitive.") (5)

truth table. A scheme for analyzing forms and relations among them. (6)

universal quantity. Refers to a form that distributes it subject. (2)

univocal. Having one meaning, not equivocal. (2, 3, 4)

unsound. See also sound. A quality of valid deductive arguments when one or more of the propositions are false. (1)

valid. A property of arguments in which the conclusion necessarily follows from the premises; an argument is valid if the form of the conclusion is true every time the forms of the premises are true. (1, 3, 4)

valid inference. An inference is valid whenever the form of the conclusion is true every time the forms of the premises are. (1, 3, 4)

Venn Diagrams. See diagrams. (4)

9 BOOKS FOR FURTHER STUDY

Recommended titles by Gordon H. Clark

Logic*

In Defense of Theology

The Johannine Logos

A Christian View of Men and Things

The Philosophy of Science and Belief in God

Thales to Dewey: A History of Philosophy

*Logic Workbook for Gordon Clark's Logic with Exercises and Answers by Elihu Carranza.

All of the above titles are published by and available from The Trinity Foundation, Post Office Box 68, Unicoi, Tennessee 37692.

Applied Logic Works by Tweedy Flynch

One Murder One

One Murder Two

One Murder Three

10 EXERCISE ANSWERS

Chapter 1: Exercise 1.1

ITEM	ANSWER
1	True
2	False
3	False
4	True
5	True
6	False
7	True
8	True
9	True
10	False

Chapter 1: Exercise 1.2

ITEM	ANSWER	
1	A	logic
2	B	law of identity
3	I (i)	law of contradiction

4	I (i)	law of contradiction
5	F	necessary inference
6	H	valid
7	I (i)	law of contradiction
8	J	unsound
9	H, G	valid, invalid
10	E	sound
11	E, J	sound, unsound
12	K	law of excluded middle

Chapter 2: Exercise 2.1

ITEM	ANSWER	
1	J	universal
2	K	particular
3	E	distributed
4	G	undistributed
5	E	distributed
6	I (i), H	quality, quantity
7	B	I(ab)
8	B	I(ab)
9	A	A(ab)
10	D	E(ab)
11	C	O(ab)
12	E, G or	distributed, undistributed; or
	G, E	undistributed, distributed

Chapter 2: Exercise 2.2

	PROPOSITION	SYMBOLIZED	FORM
1	No Christian is a secularist.	No c is s.	E(cs)

2	Some children are runners-to-school.	Some c is s.	I(sc)
3	All students who get A's are good students.	All s is g.	A(sg)
4	All those who deserve the fair are brave.	All f is b.	A(fb)
5	All non-workers are those who may enter. No worker is one who may enter.	All non-w is e. & No w is e.	A(w' s) & E(we)
6	All those who use the back door are freshmen.	All b is f.	A(bf)
7	All times someone is with you are times the poor are with you.	All w is p.	A(wp)
8	All times you get into an argument are times you squirm out of it.	All a is o.	A(ao)
9	All non-Godly labor is vain. No Godly labor is vain.	All non-l is v. & No l is v.	A(l' v) & E(lv)
10	All logic is necessary-inference-science.	All l is s.	A(ls)
11	All sinners are transgressors-of-the-law.	All s is l.	A(sl)
12	All of the Fall is a bringer-of-sin-and-misery.	All f is e.	A(fe)
13	No worthwhile thing is an easy thing.	No w is e.	E(we)
14	All lovers of instruction are lovers of knowledge.	All i is k.	A(ik)
15	No one who is in Jesus Christ is one who is condemned.	No j is c.	E(jc)
16	All of the New Testament sacraments are Baptism	All s is a.	A(sa)

	and the Lord's Supper.		
17	All those who say something meaningful are those who do so by virtue of the Law of Contradiction.	All m is l.	A(ml)
18	Some hold that God's Sovereignty and man's responsibility are paradoxical.	Some s is p.	I(sp)
19	Some exercise items are easy.	Some i is e.	I(ie)
20	Some eligible voters are non-voters. also Some eligible voters are not persons who vote.	Some e is non-v. also, Some e is not v.	I(ev′) also O(ev)

Chapter 3: Exercise 3.1

ITEM	ANSWER	
1	C	contraries
2	G	subcontraries
3	H	subalterns
4	A	contradiction
5	D	conversion
6	D	conversion
7	B	contraposition
8	F	obversion
9	E	invalid
10	I	valid
11	I	valid
12	E	invalid
13	A	contradiction

14	H	subalterns
15	F	obversion

Chapter 3: Exercise 3.2

ITEM	IMPLICATION	ANSWER
1	A(ab) < E(ab′)	valid
2	A(ab) < I(ab)	valid
3	A(ab) < O(ab′)	invalid
4	E(ab) < A(ab′)	valid
5	E(ab) < I(a′b)	invalid
6	E(ab) < O(ab)	valid
7	I(ab) < I(ba)	valid
8	I(ab) < I(b′a′)	invalid
9	I(ab) < O(ab′)	valid
10	O(ab) < A(ab′)	invalid
11	O(ab) < O(b′a′)	valid
12	O(ab) < I(ab′)	valid

Chapter 3: Exercise 3.3

ITEM	ANSWER
1	false
2	true
3	false
4	true
5	true
6	false
7	true

Chapter 4: Exercise 4.1

ITEM	ANSWER	
1	K	syllogism
2	D	major term
3	G	minor term
4	E	middle term
5	C	major premise
6	F	minor premise
7	J	simple conversion
8	A	conversion per accidens
9	B	first figure
10	I (i)	second figure
11	L	third figure
12	H	RAA reductio

Chapter 4: Exercise 4.2

1	All thinking beings are existing beings. I am a thinking being. ∴ I am an existing being.	AAA-1 Barbara (A version of Cogito, ergo sum. It is questionable whether "existence" is a significant predicate.)
2	All communists are persons who practice what they preach. Some good Christians are persons who practice what they preach. ∴ Some good Christians are communists.	AII-2, Invalid by Rule 1; the middle term is undistributed
3	All persons who are stupid are persons who swallow propaganda. No logic students are persons who are stupid. ∴ No logic students are persons who swallow propaganda.	AEE-1; Invalid, Rule 2; the major term in premise is undistributed

4	All who know the truth are free indeed. All whom the Son makes free are those who know the truth. ∴ All whom the Son makes free are free indeed.	AAA-1; Barbara, Valid
5	No thing that is a descriptive science is a thing that can justify evaluations. All psychology-science is a descriptive science. ∴ No psychology-science is a thing that can justify evaluations.	EAE-1; Celarent, Valid
6	All things done by God are good things. All God-predestinated-evil is a thing done by God. ∴ All God-predestinated-evil is a good thing.	AAA-1; Barbara, Valid
7	No person who knows the truth is a slave of sin. All whom the son makes free are persons who know the truth. ∴ No person whom the Son makes free is a slave of sin.	EAE-1; Celarent, Valid
8	All theologians are former seminary students. Some former seminary students are poor scholars. ∴ Some poor scholars are theologians.	AII-4; Invalid, Rule 1; middle term is undistributed
9	All changes in our sense organs are changes that lead to deception at one time or another. All persons are persons who have changes in their sense organs. ∴ All persons are persons who have changes that lead to deception at one time or another.	AAA-1; Barbara, Valid
10	All system-starting-points, by definition, are indemonstrable axioms. All systems of philosophy (or theology) are systems that choose starting points. ∴ All	AAA-1; Barbara, Valid

	systems of thought are systems with indemonstrable axioms.	
10	OR, No starting points of a system of thought are first principles that can be demonstrated. Every system of thought has starting points. ∴ No system of thought has first principles that can be demonstrated.	EAE-1; Celarent, Valid

Chapter 4: Exercise 4.3

ITEM	ANSWER	
1	A	axioms
2	C	Principle 1 (Deduction)
3	D	Principle 2 (Deduction)
4	E, F	e strengthened form f weakened form
5	G	Five Rules
6	B	theorem
7	H	necessary & sufficient

Chapter 5: Exercise 5.1

ITEM	ANSWER	
1	G	modus ponens
2	H	modus tollens
3	B	fallacy of affirming the consequent
4	D	fallacy of denying the antecedent
5	A	disjunctive syllogism
6	E	dilemma
7	J	valid
8	C	complete
9	I	interdefinable

10	F	transitive syllogism

Chapter 5: Exercise 5.2

ITEM	ANSWER	
1	Invalid	Fallacy of Affirming the Consequent
2	Invalid	Fallacy of Denying the Antecedent
3	Valid	Transitive Syllogism
4	Valid	Modus Ponens
5	Invalid	Fallacy of Affirming the Consequent
6	Valid	Transitive Syllogism using interdefinability of disjunction & implication with premises.
7	Valid*	Constructive Dilemma*
8	Valid	Disjunctive Syllogism, or Modus Tollens using disjunction & implication interdefinability
9	Valid	Valid, Interdefinability of implication, disjunction, & conjunction
10	Valid	Valid, Interdefinability of disjunction & conjunction

(*Valid only if it meets all the conditions of a genuine dilemma; otherwise, Invalid.)

Chapter 6: Review Exercise

(1) Either the birds are singing or the baby is crying.

(2) If the baby is not crying, then the wind is blowing.

(3) Either the birds are not singing or the wind is not blowing.

(4) [If the baby is crying, then the wind is not blowing.]

Questions: Are the birds singing? Is the baby crying? Is the wind blowing? (Gordon H. Clark. *Logic*, HC ed., p. 106, Brackets mine).

Let S = the birds are singing; C = the baby is crying; B = the wind is blowing.

VARIABLES				#1	#2	#3	#4
	S	C	B	S∨C	C′<B	S′∨B′	C<B′
1	T	T	T	T	T	F	F
2	T	T	F	T	T	T	T
3	T	F	T	T	T	F	T
4	T	F	F	T	F	T	T
5	F	T	T	T	T	T	F
6	F	T	F	T	T	T	T
7	F	F	T	F	T	T	T
8	F	F	F	F	F	T	T
	i	ii	iii	iv	v	vi	vii

In what rows are columns (iv) to (vii) all true? Only rows 2 and 6 show true for columns (iv), (v), (vi), and (vii). In rows 2 and 6, variable S is true and false; therefore, nothing can be said about "singing birds." In rows 2 and 6, variable *C* is true both times; therefore, it is true that "the baby is crying." In rows 2 and 6 variable *B* is false both times; therefore, it is false that "the wind is blowing."

Chapter 6: Exercise 6.1

Part A: Match Part A truth table values in the columns with the correct Forms 1 through 7.

X	Y	A	B	C	D	E	F	G
T	T	T	T	F	F	T	F	F
T	F	F	F	T	T	T	F	F
F	T	T	F	T	F	T	F	T
F	F	T	F	T	F	F	T	T

	FORM	ANSWER
1	conjunction	B
2	disjunction	E

3	implication	A
4	contradiction of conjunction	C
5	contradiction of disjunction	F
6	contradiction of implication	D
7	contradiction of variable X.	G

Part B: Match Part B truth table values in the columns with the correct Expressions 1 through 10.

p	q	A	B	C	D	E	F	G
T	T	T	F	F	T	T	T	F
T	F	T	F	T	F	F	T	F
F	T	T	F	T	T	F	F	F
F	F	T	F	T	T	F	F	T

	EXPRESSION	ANSWER
1	$(p \lor q)'$	G
2	$(pp')'$	A
3	$(p \lor p')'$	B
4	$(pq)'$	C
5	$(p' \lor q)$	D
6	$(pq')'$	D
7	$(p' \lor q')$	C
8	$(p' \lor q')'$	E
9	$(p < p')'$	F
10	$(p' \lor p')'$	F

Chapter 6: Exercise 6.2

What do these four propositions imply? Is Hawk good in anything? In or at what?

Hawk is good in either science or theology, but not both. Moreover, either he is good at logic or bad at theology. If he is not good in science, he is bad at theology. If he is bad at theology, he is good at logic.

1	Hawk is good in either science or theology, but not both.	$(s \lor t)\,(s\,t)'$
2	Hawk is good at logic or bad at theology.	$(l \lor t')$
3	If he is not good in science, he is bad at theology.	$(s' < t')$
4	If he is bad at theology, he is good at logic.	$(t' < l)$

	VARIABLES			1st		2nd	3rd	4th
	s	l	t	$s \lor t$	$(st)'$	$l \lor t'$	$s' < t'$	$t' < l$
1	T	T	T	T	F	T	T	T
2	T	T	F	T	T	T	T	T
3	T	F	T	T	F	F	T	T
4	T	F	F	T	T	T	T	F
5	F	T	T	T	T	T	F	T
6	F	T	F	F	T	T	T	T
7	F	F	T	T	T	F	F	T
8	F	F	F	F	T	T	T	F
	i	ii	iii	iv	v	vi	vii	viii

Row #2 is the only row that has true values in columns (iv) through (viii).

Notice the values of the propositional variables in that same row. There, Hawk is good at science and logic, but it is false that he is good at theology, at least according to this truth table analysis.

Although these propositions are not premises of an argument with a conclusion, a valid deduction is possible from the third and fourth propositions.

[(s' < t') and (t' < l)] imply (s' < l) by transitive syllogism. If Hawk is not good at science, then he is good at logic.

Chapter 7: Exercise 7.1

ITEM	ANSWER
1	True
2	False
3	True
4	False
5	True
6	False
7	True
8	False
9	True
10	False
11	True
12	True
13	False
14	False
15	True

Chapter 7: Exercise 7.2

ITEM	ANSWER	NAME
1	B	argumentum ad baculum
2	C	argumentum ad hominem, abusive
3	D	argumentum ad ignorantiam
4	F	argumentum ad populum
5	G	argumentum ad verecundiam

6	O	false dilemma
7	P	None of the Above (hasty generalization)
8	J	circular reasoning
9	E	argumentum ad misericordiam
10	H	equivocation
11	I	amphibology
12	A	accent (emphasis)
13	L	composition
14	N	post hoc
15	M	division

Chapter 7: Exercise 7.3

ITEM	ANSWER	NAME
1	F	lexical
2	K	stipulative
3	J	precising
4	M	theoretical
5	I	persuasive
6	B, C	denotative, designative
7	B	denotative
8	L	synonymous
9	A	analytic
10	E	genus & difference
11	D	genetic
12	G	operational

ABOUT THE AUTHOR

Elihu Carranza, Ph.D., Professor Emeritus, San Jose State University, taught courses in Philosophy, Logic, Argumentation, and Humanities. While on leave from the University, he was Provost, Evergreen Valley College in San Jose, California. He lives in Napa, California.

Made in the USA
Coppell, TX
08 August 2020

32746089R00085